Caroline H. Harding

The City of the Seven Hills

A book of stories from the history of ancient Rome

Caroline H. Harding

The City of the Seven Hills
A book of stories from the history of ancient Rome

ISBN/EAN: 9783337380366

Printed in Europe, USA, Canada, Australia, Japan

Cover: Foto ©ninafisch / pixelio.de

More available books at **www.hansebooks.com**

THE
CITY OF THE SEVEN HILLS

*A Book of Stories from the History of
Ancient Rome*

BY

CAROLINE H. HARDING, A.B.

AND

SAMUEL B. HARDING, Ph.D.
Associate Professor of History in Indiana University

CHICAGO
SCOTT, FORESMAN AND COMPANY
1898

PREFACE.

In this volume, the attempt has been made to give a picture of the life and history of the Roman people. So far as it has been feasible, this has been done by means of biographical sketches, selected so as to be illustrative of the Roman character, its virtues and its faults. In this way, it has also been possible to weave into the narrative a more vivid description of the daily life and customs of the men, women and children of Rome, than would have been the case under any other method of treatment. In the last chapter, an attempt is made to relate the old Rome to modern life through a description of some existing remains, and to point out in a few words the way in which the ancient city was merged in the Rome of to-day.

In a work designed for young children, as is this one, it seems desirable that the brutal element of Roman character and history should be eliminated so far as is possible; and to this end, much has been omitted from the narrative which might properly find a place in a history of Rome for High School use.

The limited view which is here offered, however, is a fundamentally true one, and it may easily be developed into the accurate historical idea when the proper time comes for more advanced study.

The book is designed especially for use as a supplementary reader for children of the sixth and seventh grades. Inasmuch, however, as some teachers may wish to use it for formal instruction in history, the book has been equipped with maps, summaries of chapters, and a chronological analysis of Roman history. In this way, it is hoped that its use as a textbook may be facilitated without robbing it of its attractiveness as a reader.

BLOOMINGTON, INDIANA.
November, 1898.

TABLE OF CONTENTS.

CHAP.		PAGE
	Preface	3
	List of Illustrations	6
I.	The Peninsula of Italy	7
II.	Romulus and the Beginning of Rome	15
III.	Numa, the Peaceful King	22
IV.	The Last of the Kings	30
V.	The War with Lars Porsena	36
VI.	The Stories of Mucius and Clœlia	43
VII.	Secession of the Plebeians	49
VIII.	The Story of Coriolanus	55
IX.	The Family of the Fabii	62
X.	The Victory of Cincinnatus	68
XI.	The Laws of the Twelve Tables	74
XII.	How Camillus Captured Veii	80
XIII.	The Coming of the Gauls	87
XIV.	The Gauls in Rome	94
XV.	Rebuilding the City	101
XVI.	The New Rome	110
XVII.	The War with Pyrrhus	118
XVIII.	Rome and the Carthaginians	128
XIX.	The War with Hannibal	138
XX.	Rome Conquers the World	150
XXI.	The Gracchi and their Mother	161
XXII.	The Wars of Caius Marius	169
XXIII.	Cicero, the Orator	176
XXIV.	Julius Cæsar, the Conqueror of Gaul	189
XXV.	Cæsar and the Beginning of the Empire	204
XXVI.	Rome in the Time of Augustus	217
XXVII.	The Empire after Augustus	229
XXVIII.	The Christians and the Empire	236
XXIX.	The Remains of Ancient Rome	244
	Summaries of Chapters	257
	Chronological Outline	265
	Index	268

The City of the Seven Hills.

I

The Peninsula of Italy.

IF you will look at a map of Europe, you will see three great peninsulas extending from its southern coast into the Mediterranean Sea. The one which lies farthest to the east is the peninsula of Greece; you may have read of its beautiful scenery, and the brave people who lived there in olden times. The peninsula farthest to the west, with the Atlantic Ocean washing its rocky coast, is Spain. The land lying between the two is Italy; and it was there that a great people lived, many centuries ago, whose story you are now to read.

These three peninsulas of southern Europe differ greatly from one another in shape and size. The Grecian peninsula is not nearly so large as that of Spain or Italy, and it has a number of smaller peninsulas running out into the surrounding seas like the stubby fingers of a great hand. Spain is the largest of the three, and it is almost square in shape, with few bays and capes along its coast-line. Italy, which lies between the two in position, is also between the two in size and shape. It is larger than Greece, and smaller than Spain, and its coast line is neither so broken as that of the former, nor so regular as that of the latter. In shape, Italy is long and slender, and very much like a huge boot. On the map you will see it lying in the midst of the Mediterranean, with its toe to the south and its heel to the east; and if you will look closely you will see that there is a great spur, too, upon the back of the boot,—but, instead of being placed on the heel, it has slipped far up on the ankle.

The peninsula of Italy lies about as far north on the earth's surface as the State of New York, but it has a very different climate from that which is found in this latitude in America. To the north of it lies a high chain of mountains, which protect its sunny plains from the cold northern winds; while the sea that lies around it is warmed by the hot currents of air from the deserts of Africa. In this way, the winters are made milder, and the summers warmer, than with us, so that the orange and the olive grow there, where the people of our own country raise the pear and the apple.

The surface of Italy varies greatly in different parts of the peninsula. In the northern part, between the steep wall of the Alps and the mountains to the south of them, lies a broad, well-watered plain, larger than the State of Indiana. Here we find the most fertile land in all Europe, where grow great fields of wheat and other grain, and groves of waving mulberry trees. Here, too, is to be found the largest river of Italy—the River Po—which draws its waters from the melting snows of the Alps and flows eastward to the Adriatic Sea.

South of the basin of the Po, we come to a belt of

mountains again. These are the Apennines. They are not nearly so high as the snowy Alps, but still they

are higher in many places than the tallest peaks of our Appalachians. From where they leave the Alps, the Apennines sweep eastward almost across the peninsula;

then they gradually curve to the southward and extend to the very toe of the peninsula. This same range appears again in Sicily, and forms the backbone of that island. Among these mountains we may see many lofty peaks, covered to the very top with forests of chestnut, oak and pine. Between the parallel ridges of the chain lie pleasant valleys without number; and at their foot are broad uplands where herds and flocks can find pasture in the hottest and driest summer weather.

On both sides of this wooded mountain chain, plains and wide belts of marshy country stretch away to the sea. On the eastern side, the slope is quite steep and short, and the land there is hilly and broken by deep gorges through which the rivers have cut their way to the Adriatic. Only people who live, for the most part, on the products of their sheep, goats and cattle, can find a living here. On the western side, the slope is more gentle, and broad, fertile plains lie between the mountains and the sea. Here the people do not have to depend so largely on their flocks and herds, for they can raise grain, and grow vineyards; and, in the south, groves of orange, fig and olive trees may be seen.

As the peninsula is so narrow and the slopes so short, you could not expect to find long, deep rivers, in that part of the country which lies south of the River Po. Many streams rise in the mountains, and flow down across the country into the sea, but they are most of them short, and few of them are deep enough to bear a ship, or even a boat of large size. They vary, however, according to the season of the year. Sometimes, after the rains have begun to fall, or when the snow is melting on the tops of the mountains, they are rushing torrents which sweep everything before them. Then, again, when the summer heats have come, and the rains have ceased, they shrink to little, harmless streams, or dry up altogether. The only river, south of the basin of the Po, which is deep enough to bear boats and small ships all the year around is the Tiber. This river rises in the Apennines, where they bend to the south; it follows a long course through the plains, and then flows into the Mediterranean about half-way down the western side of the peninsula. The waters of even this longer river vary greatly at different seasons of the year, and its swift current is so often muddied with floods from rains and melting snows that it has been called "the yellow Tiber."

Now that we have seen the surface of the peninsula of Italy, suppose that we go aboard a ship and sail along its shores in order to get an idea of its coast. We will begin our journey at the point farthest to the west. Here the Alps and the Apennines run together, and the mountains lie close to the water's edge. The shores are steep and lofty, and in many places there is barely room for a road to run between the mountains and the sea.

Sailing from here across the gulf which lies between the peninsula and the mainland, we come to a coast where the Apennines leave the shore and are lost to sight to the eastward. This part of the coast is not so mountainous, but still it is high and rocky. As we go southward, however, it gradually becomes lower, until we see the flat and marshy plains that lie about the mouth of the Tiber. Let us look well, as we pass, at that broad, flat plain that lies south of the Tiber; for it was there, many centuries ago, that the people lived of whom we are to read.

When we have sailed past this low-lying coast, we come again to a bold and rocky shore. Here the coast-line is cut into broad, deep bays, whose shores are dotted with towns which were founded long, long ago. Towering above the waters of one of these bays we see the smoking summit of Mount Vesuvius, one of the most famous volcanoes in the world.

From here, all around the toe of Italy, the sea is faced by steep rocks, behind which rise lofty heights. On the shores of the great gulf which lies between the toe and the heel of the peninsula, we find another broad, well-watered plain; and here too are cities which were founded in the ancient days.

As we sail around the eastern corner of the peninsula, we look out upon a low and sandy country, which makes up the heel of the boot. As we continue up the eastern shore, we notice that there are almost no good harbors on this side of the peninsula. We do not need to be told, therefore, that in ancient times there were few cities here, and that only shepherds and cattle-raisers lived on the rolling plains.

In some places this eastern shore is high also, and in others we find long stretches of low and sandy country. When we reach the land about the mouth of the River Po, we see wide, unhealthy marshes and many small sandy islands. Upon a group of these islands, the wonderful city of Venice is now built; but in the times of which you are now to read, there was no Venice, and all these islands were either marshy wastes, or the homes of a few scattered fishermen.

In this peninsula of Italy, which we have been examining so carefully, there now lives a nation of people who are united under one king into a government called the kingdom of Italy. But when our story begins, about seven hundred and fifty years before Christ was born, there was no kingdom of Italy and no Italian nation.

Instead of this, there were many separate groups of people living in the peninsula, who were only distantly related, and who had very little to do with each other. They knew much less about their country than we do now; for there were no books then to tell them about it, and in every direction the mountains, the rivers, or the sea hemmed them in, and made traveling so difficult that they could not well find out about it for themselves. So it happened, that most of these peoples were acquainted only with the groups who lived close by them; and they were interested only in their own little city, and in their farms and pasture-lands which lay about it.

In those olden days, each little city had its own king, who governed the people in time of peace, and led them in war, when they fought against their neighbors. Often, when there came to be too many people to live comfortably within the walls of a city, the younger and the poorer people would go away from their old homes and begin a new city somewhere else.

Each of these new cities, like the old one, would be built on a hill or some high place which could easily be defended against their enemies. There the people would build their fort—or citadel, as they called it—and the rest of the town would grow up about it. Then, from their homes in this strong place, the people would go into the surrounding country to cultivate their farms and to herd their cattle; but to this spot they would always retreat in time of danger. In this way every town lived more or less to itself, obeying its own king, fighting its own battles, and owning and cultivating a few miles of land about it.

In very early times, there was one city of this sort, on the south bank of the River Tiber, about twenty miles from the sea. It was called Rome, and at first it was probably not very different from a hundred other towns in Italy. As time went on, however, Rome was to become much more than this. It was to conquer, first, the cities that lay nearest to it. Then it was to conquer those which lay farther and farther away, until it had made all Italy its own. Then it was to reach out, and conquer all of the lands about the Mediterranean Sea. In this way, it was to become, at last, the mightiest city that the world has ever seen.

II

Romulus and the Beginning of Rome.

WE do not know just when, or how, or by whom the first beginning of Rome was made. It happened so long ago, and so few people could write in those early days, that no account, written at the time, has come down to us. Indeed, it is very likely that nobody then dreamed that the world would ever care to know how this little city was first commenced.

But, after Rome had begun to grow, and to conquer her neighbors, and people had begun to read and write more, then the Romans themselves began to be curious to know about the beginning of their city. It was too late to find out then, for the persons who had been alive at the time that it was founded were now long dead and forgotten. But the Romans continued to wonder about it, and at last they made up many stories of the early years of their city; and they came to believe these stories themselves, and have handed them down to us who have come after them.

According to these stories, the first settlers at Rome came from a little city named Alba Longa; and the way they happened to leave that place and settle at Rome was this.

The rightful king of Alba Longa had been put out of power by his brother. Then this brother had killed the true **king's sons, and shut his** daughter up in prison; and there the princess had given birth to beautiful twin sons. When **her cruel** uncle heard this, and saw how large and strong the children were, he was much troubled; **for he** feared that, if they should grow up to be men, they might some day take his **ill-gotten** throne **from** him. He determined, therefore, **to** put them to death; so he took the sleeping children in the wooden trough which served as their cradle, **and** gave them to a servant, and told him to drown them in the River Tiber.

The river **at this time was** overflowing its banks, and the main current **ran so swift and** strong that the **man was afraid to go near the bed of the** stream. For **this** reason, he **merely set the** trough down in the shallow water at the river's edge, **and went** his way. There the children floated gently, for some time, while their cradle was carried by the waters to a place where seven low hills formed the southern bank of the stream. The river was now going down as rapidly as it had risen; and here, at the foot of a wild fig **tree** which grew at the base of one of these hills, the cradle at last caught in a vine and **came** safely **to land.**

In this way the children escaped drowning, but they were still alone and uncared for, far from the homes of men. Soon, however, they were provided for in a wonderful manner. When they began to cry of hunger, a mother wolf that had **lost** its cubs came to them, and gave them milk; and a woodpecker flew **down** from the trees and brought them food.

In this way the children lived for some time. At last a shepherd of Alba Longa, who had often watched the wolf coming and going from the place, found the boys and saw how they had been cared for. The Italians thought that wolves and woodpeckers were sacred to Mars, their god of war; so this shepherd had no doubt that the children were favorites of that god. He took them up, therefore, and brought them to his little hut, and he and his wife named the boys Romulus and Remus, and adopted them as their own.

As they grew up among the shepherd people, Romulus and Remus became strong and brave, and showed spirits that nothing could subdue. Whenever there was a hunting party, or a contest in running or wrestling, or a struggle with robbers, who tried to drive off their flocks and herds, Romulus and Remus were sure to be among the foremost.

In this way, they won great fame among the shepherds, but they also gained the hatred of evil-doers. At last, some lawless men, in revenge, seized Remus at a festival, and bore him to the false king of Alba Longa, and charged him with robbery. There the true king saw the young man, and he was struck with his appearance, and questioned him about his birth, but Remus could tell him little.

In the meantime, the shepherd who had found the boys told Romulus the whole story of the finding of himself and Remus; and Romulus gathered together a company of his companions, and hurried to the city to save his brother. In this he soon succeeded; and then the two brothers joined together to punish the cruel king of Alba Longa, and to set their newly-found grandfather on his throne once more.

After this, the brothers were not willing to remain

in Alba Longa unless they could govern there, and yet they did not wish to take the government from their grandfather. As there were now more people in the city of Alba Longa than could live comfortably within its walls, it was decided to build a new city under the leadership of Romulus and Remus; and the two brothers decided to build the city near the fig tree, where they had been found as children by their foster-father.

This was an excellent place for a city. On the nearest hill, which was called the Palatine, they could build their citadel; and at its foot were valleys in which they could plant their grain. If they wanted to trade with other cities, there was the River Tiber near at hand, for their boats to come and go upon; and, if, at any time, the city should grow too large for this one small hill, there were the six other hills near by to which the city might spread.

After Romulus and Remus had decided upon the place for their city, a difficulty arose. A new city must have a founder, who should give his name to it; but which of the brothers should have this honor? As they were both of the same age, and could not settle the matter by giving the honor to the elder, they agreed to leave the choice to the gods of the place. So each took his stand upon one of the hills to receive a sign from the gods by watching the flight of birds. Then Remus saw six vultures from his hill-top; but Romulus, a little later, saw twelve. This was thought to be a better sign than that of Remus; so Romulus became the founder of the new city, and it was called Rome after him.

Then Romulus began to mark off the boundaries of the city. He did this by hitching a bull and a cow to a plough, and drawing a deep furrow about the hill. After that they raised a wall about the place, and Romulus invited to his city all persons who might wish to come and settle there. And many of his rude shepherd friends and many of the young men of Alba settled there with him; and men from other places, both slaves and freemen, joined them from time to time.

In this way there were soon enough men in the city to make it a match for its neighbors in war. But still there were few women in the town, for the neighboring people would not allow their daughters to be taken in marriage by the runaway slaves and rude herdsmen of Rome.

At last, Romulus planned to get by a trick what he could not get by fair means. He made a great festival in honor of the gods, and invited the people of the cities near at hand, and especially those of the tribe of the Sabines, to come and behold the games that were to take place. The people came, bringing their sisters and their daughters with them; then, while the visitors were intently watching the spectacle, the young men of Rome suddenly seized upon the young women and carried them off to their homes to be their wives.

Of course, this broke up the festival, and the visitors left Rome, furiously angry at the wrong that had been done them. The men of Rome soon found that they must fight to keep the wives that they had taken by force.

At first, it was only the people of the cities near at

hand that came against them, and these the Romans easily defeated. But soon the powerful Sabine tribe, with their king at their head, came against Rome; and then the Romans were not so successful. First a fort, which the Romans had built on the hill called the Capitol, fell into the hands of the Sabines. Then, on the next day, the Romans and the Sabines met in battle in the valley between the Capitol and their city. The fight raged fiercely for a long time. First one side, and then the other, seemed victorious; but the battle still went on.

At last, the captive Sabine women took courage to interfere and stop the bloodshed. They threw themselves between the weapons of their fathers and their brothers on the one side, and those of their newly-made husbands on the other; and they implored them to cease the fight, as it must bring sorrow to them, no matter who became the victors.

Then the battle ceased, and the leaders of the Sabines, moved by the appeal of the women, came forward to make peace. It was agreed that the Romans should keep their wives, and that the Sabines should go to Rome to live, and that the two peoples should share the city between them.

From this time the city grew rapidly, and it soon spread to others of the seven hills by the Tiber. Its people became so strong in war that none of their neighbors could harm them; and in war and in peace, Romulus was their leader, and was greatly beloved by the people. He made many laws for them and established many good customs. He ordered that every eighth day there should be a market held at Rome, at which the country folk might sell their produce; and he himself heard cases and dealt out justice there in the market place. And to aid him in the government, he formed a council of the older and wiser men, which was called the Senate, or the council of the city fathers.

In this way, Romulus ruled his people for thirty-seven years. Then, one day, as he was reviewing the army, a sudden darkness fell upon the earth, and a mighty storm of thunder and lightning came upon them. When this had passed, and the air was clear once more, Romulus could nowhere be seen.

While the citizens were seeking their king, and mourning for him, a citizen came forward, who said that, in the midst of the storm, he had seen Romulus carried up to heaven in the chariot of his father, Mars. After that the people ceased to mourn for him, for they now believed that he had become a god, and from that time on they not only honored him as the founder of their city, but they worshiped him as one of the gods of heaven.

III
Numa, the Peaceful King.

AFTER Romulus had been taken from them, the Romans at first could not agree as to who should be king in his place. The citizens who had first settled there wished to choose a king from their own number again; but the Sabines objected to this. They said that they had faithfully obeyed Romulus while he lived, and that now it was their turn to have a king chosen from among themselves.

For a long time, the two parties could not come to an agreement. In the meantime, the Senate took the place of a king, and carried on the government itself. This, however, did not please the people. They said that now they had many kings, instead of one; and they demanded that a real king should be chosen. At last, it was arranged that the old citizens should choose a king from among the Sabines; and Numa was then chosen to rule in the place of Romulus.

The new king was different from Romulus in many ways. Romulus had been a great soldier, and he had trained the people of the city for war; but, during his time, the men of Rome had little time or thought to give to anything else. It seemed to King Numa that there were other things which were of more importance than the knowledge of war, and the art of winning battles. He saw, too, that the Romans were too harsh and violent, as warlike people always are; and he wished to soften their manners and make them less rude.

So King Numa made peace with all the enemies of Rome; and, during the three and forty years that he ruled, there was no war. This left the Romans free to till their fields, and learn the arts of peace; and to encourage them in this, Numa divided among the citizens the lands which Romulus had won in war. King Numa ruled his people as a wise and peaceful king; but, better than this, he also taught the Romans how to honor their gods.

The Romans believed in many gods,—indeed, almost every thing, and every act, was looked upon by them as having a god to watch over it. In later times, when they came to know the Greeks, they confused their own gods with the gods of the Greeks; and still later, they sometimes borrowed gods from other peoples with whom they came in contact. So, if we tried to write down all the gods that the Romans believed in, it would make a very long list indeed, and not a very interesting one. But there were some of the gods that were very important in the life of the Romans, and you ought to know about these.

The chief of the gods was Jupiter, the "Sky-father," whom they called the "Best and Greatest." He sent forth the clouds and ruled the storm, and the thunderbolt was his weapon. It was he, too, who sent the birds whose flight showed the will of the gods to men; and Victory and Good Faith were his constant companions.

Next to Jupiter (or Jove, as he was sometimes

called), the Romans worshiped Mars, the god of war. He was also the god who kept off sickness from the cattle, and blight and disease from the growing grain. They also worshiped the goddess Juno, as the com-

JUPITER.

panion of Jupiter, and the queen of the sky. It was she, they thought, who cared for the Roman women, and made their children strong and vigorous. Minerva was the goddess of wisdom and inventions. She taught men the use of numbers; and each year the priest solemnly drove a nail into her temple, so that they might in this way keep count of the years as they passed; on her festival, too, the school children had holiday, for she was the goddess of schools and learning. Vesta, the goddess of the hearth-fire and of the home, was also worshiped by the Romans, and that too in a special way, as you shall see in a little while.

Last of all, there was a curious god of Beginnings, called Janus, to whom the Romans sacrificed whenever they began anything new. The first month of the year was called in his honor "January," or the month of Janus. He was especially the god of gateways; and when the Romans wished to represent him, they made a figure with two faces on one head, to show that, as the guardian of the gate, Janus looked in both directions. When the Romans were at war with any people, the gates of his temple stood open, but when they were at peace, they were closed; and during all the reign of Numa, the gates of Janus were fast shut.

The Romans already believed in these gods when Numa became king; but he showed them more clearly the way in which each god was to be worshiped. He seemed so wise in these matters, that the Romans believed that one of the gods themselves must teach him. At last it was whispered that he was often seen to wander forth to a sacred grove where dwelt a nymph, or mountain spirit, named Egeria; and the Romans believed that this nymph loved him and advised him as to what would be pleasing to each of the gods.

One of the things that Numa did was to divide the priests up into different companies, or colleges, and give each company its own part in the worship of the gods. In this way, he set apart separate priests for the worship of Jove and Mars and Romulus; and the chiefs of these priests, together with the king, were the high priests of Rome, and had charge of all things connected with the gods. A college of sacred heralds was also formed, whose business it should be to make a solemn declaration of war when the Romans took up arms against an enemy, and to proclaim the treaty of peace when the war was at an end.

For the worship of the goddess Vesta, Numa formed a company of virgins, or maidens, whose number was set at six. It was their duty to offer prayers each day, in the circular temple of the goddess; and, above all, they must take care that the holy fire which burned upon Vesta's altar was never allowed to die out.

Only the daughters of the noblest families of Rome could be appointed for this service; and they could not be chosen before they were six years old, nor after they were ten. When a Vestal Virgin was appointed, she was taken to the house of the Vestals, where she must live for the next thirty years. The first ten years she spent in learning the duties of her office; the next ten years she practiced what she had learned, and the last ten she taught their duties to the newly-made Vestals. When the thirty years were past, she might leave the Vestals, and marry and have a home of her own, if she wished; but she rarely did so. Great honor was shown them by the Romans, and if a criminal, who was being led away to imprisonment, met a Vestal Virgin by chance, he was at once set free.

There was one other company of priests, which arose

VESTAL VIRGINS.

in a peculiar way, and had very curious duties. These were the "dancing priests" of Mars, and the Roman writers say that they arose in the following manner:

In the eighth year of Numa's reign, a great sickness came upon the Romans; and while the people were much discouraged on this account, suddenly a shield of brass fell from the heavens at the feet of King Numa. When he consulted the nymph Egeria about it, she told him that it was the shield of Mars; and that the god had sent it down for the preservation of the city and that it should be kept with great care.

Then King Numa ordered that eleven other shields just like this one should be made; so that, if an enemy of the Roman people should attempt to steal the shield of Mars, he might not be able to tell the true from the false. This was done, and then King Numa appointed twelve young men of the noblest families to take the shields in charge; and he appointed a yearly festival which they should keep in honor of the god.

Each year, when March—the month of Mars—came around, these priests were to take the sacred shields, and go leaping and dancing through the streets of the city, singing old songs in his honor. This festival lasted for twenty-four days, and each day the procession came to an end at some appointed place. Then the shields were taken into one of the houses near by, and there the dancing priests were entertained with a fine supper.

Numa also ordered that whenever a war should break out, and it should be necessary for a Roman army to march out to battle, the general should first go to the altar of the war-god, and strike the sacred shields and cry out:

"Awake, Mars, and watch over us!"

Then—so the Romans believed—the god would answer their appeal by going unseen before the army as it marched to battle; and in later days stories were told of times when the god appeared in the form of a young man to encourage the soldiers, and lead them on when they were in danger of being defeated.

In this way, King Numa arranged the worship of the different gods. By the sacrifices, religious dances, and processions which he appointed, he made the worship pleasant and agreeable to the people. So they followed the rules which he laid down for them, and, in the course of time, the Romans began to lose some of the fierceness which had marked the first rude settlers.

At last, after many years of quiet rule, King Numa died peacefully of old age, and all the nations about Rome so honored the memory of this king that they sent crowns and offerings to his funeral.

IV

The Last of the Kings.

AFTER the death of Numa, the long peace which Rome had enjoyed came to an end. Under the kings who followed him, the wars with her neighbors were renewed, and it was centuries before the gates of the temple of Janus again stood closed. Some of these rulers were more peaceful than others, but all were good warriors. So the Romans were usually successful in their wars, and the land which Rome ruled grew larger, bit by bit, by their conquests. Above all, the Romans learned two lessons in these times. They learned to fight well and bravely; and they learned to obey their rulers in war and in peace.

After a number of years, trouble arose between Rome and Alba Longa, its mother city. War followed, and the men of Alba were defeated. Then it was agreed that the people of that city should leave their homes and seek new ones at Rome; and the city of Alba Longa was destroyed.

The settlers who came from Alba Longa, at this time, were so numerous that the population of Rome was nearly doubled by their coming. As the city grew, the hills about the Palatine had been occupied, one after the other, and now Rome could truly be called "the City of the Seven Hills." As the city grew, it became necessary to defend these new parts, also, against Rome's enemies. At last, new walls of stone were built for the city, and all of the seven hills of Rome were included within them. So large was the space which they inclosed, that for many hundreds of

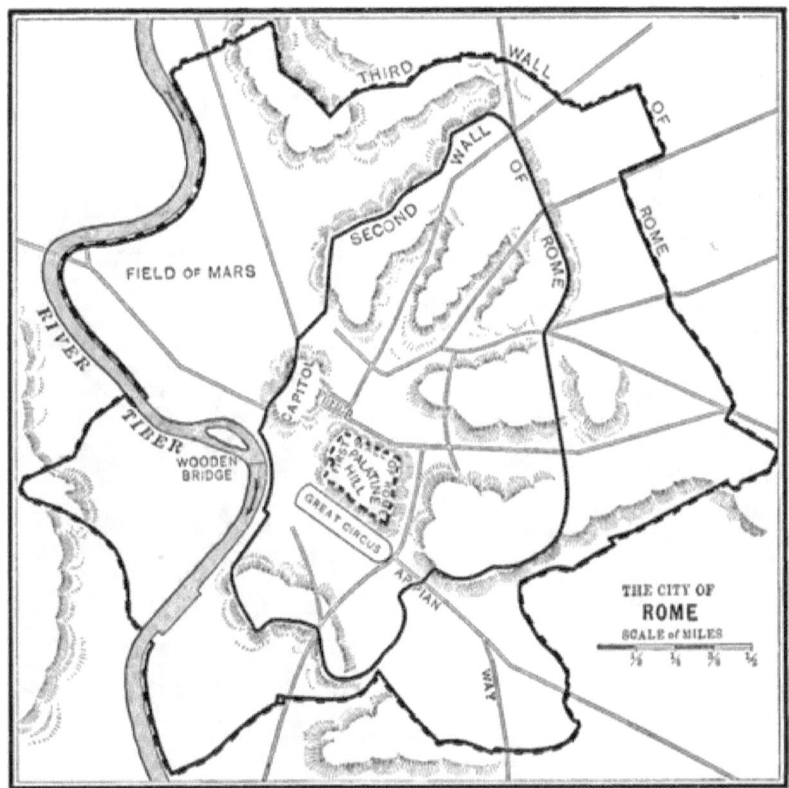

years the city did not outgrow them; and so well was the work done in building them, that parts of these walls are still standing to this day.

Many other useful public works were built at this time. The valleys between the hills of the city were low and marshy in places; to drain these, and make them healthy and fit for men to dwell in, great **sewers** were built which emptied their waters into the River Tiber. In one of the valleys, also, a **race-course was** laid out, **for the** chariot races, **of which the** Romans were very fond.

On **the hill called the** Capitol, a great temple was built **in honor of the** three **gods,** Jupiter, Juno, and Minerva; and this temple **stood as** the chief center of the **Roman** worship **until it** was burned, five hundred **years later.** It was so large that it covered eight acres **of ground.** Its gates were of brass, covered with gold; **while the** inside was of marble **and was** decorated **with** gold **and silver** ornaments. **When the** workmen were laying **its** foundations, **they had to remove a** number of altars **that** had **already been set up** there; but the altar **of the god of** Youth, and that **of the god of Boundaries, they** could not move. Then the priests **said that this was** a sign that Rome should ever remain young **and** strong, and that her boundaries should never **be** moved backward; **so the two** altars **were** allowed to remain, and they were inclosed in the new temple.

While this great temple was still unfinished, an old, old woman came one day to the king **of** Rome. She brought **with** her nine **"books,"** or rolls of paper, in which **were** written down oracles or prophecies. **These** told how the wrath of the gods might **be turned** away, whenever it had brought sickness, famine, **or** other misfortune, on the people. **She** offered to sell the books to the king; but the price which she asked for them was so high that he refused to buy.

Then the old woman went away, and burned three of the books. When she returned, she offered him the six books that remained, but she asked for them the price which she had before asked for the nine. Again the king refused to buy. Once more the old woman burned three of the books; then she returned, and again she offered the king the ones that remained for the price she had at first asked for all.

This time the king yielded. He bought the three books at the price which she asked; and when the temple on the Capitol was finished, they were placed in a vault under it for safe keeping. After this, whenever any trouble came upon the city, one of the first things that the Romans did was to consult these books; and the message which the priests found in them, the people accepted as the voice of the gods.

After many years, the seventh king sat on the throne of Rome, and men called him Tarquin the Proud. He was a cruel and wicked man. He had gained his power by bloodshed and violence, and he used it like a tyrant. He repealed the good laws which had been made under the kings who had ruled before him, and he made others in their place. The nobles complained that he did everything by his own will, and never asked the Senate for its advice and assistance; and the people murmured at the constant wars which he carried on, and the hard tasks to which he set them in time of peace. At last, all Rome was weary of his rule, and the people of the city only needed a leader to turn against him.

This leader they found in a noble named Brutus, who had suffered much at the hands of the king. His brother had been put to death by Tarquin; and Brutus, to save himself from a like fate, had been obliged to give up his property and pretend to be dull and slow of mind, so that the king might find nothing in him to fear.

But Brutus's dulness of mind was only pretended. Once he had been sent as the companion of the king's sons when they went to consult the great Oracle at Delphi, in Greece. After finishing the business upon which they had been sent, the young men asked the Oracle which one of them should succeed King Tarquin as ruler of Rome. The Oracle replied, that he who should first kiss his mother upon their return should rule the city. When they returned to Italy, each of the princes hurried off to find their mother, in order that he might kiss her first, and so gain the throne. But Brutus understood the Oracle better. As he landed from the ship, he pretended to stumble and fall, and so kissed the ground beneath him. He guessed that the Oracle had not meant a person at all, but the great Earth, the mother of us all.

Tarquin might, perhaps, have been king of Rome until he died, if it had not been for the great wickedness of one of his sons. While Tarquin was away from the city, carrying on a war with a neighboring people, this son caused the death of a noble Roman lady named Lucretia. Because of his act, her husband and her father were filled with grief and rage. Brutus, who was with them, now threw off his pretended dulness. He seized the bloody dagger that had slain Lucretia, and swore with them that he would never rest until the family of Tarquin had ceased to reign at Rome. In order that all might see what cause they had to turn against their king, they laid the dead body of Lucretia in the market-place of the little town where she had been slain. Then Brutus hastened to Rome, and told the story there. At once the people were filled with anger against Tarquin and his sons. When the king and his followers returned to Rome, they found the gates of the city closed against them; and, in spite of all that he could do, Tarquin was never again to come within the city walls.

After they had cast out the Tarquins, the people took an oath that they would never, from that time on, allow any one to become king in Rome. One of the first things which they then had to do was to find some other form of rule, to take the place of the old one; for unless they had a settled government, their enemies would be able to overcome their armies, and King Tarquin would return to his throne once more.

So the people set up a republic. They agreed that two men, called consuls, should be elected each year; and these consuls, with the Senate, should rule Rome in the place of the kings. When the vote was taken for the consuls for the first year, it was found that Brutus was one of the two men who were elected; so the oracle was fulfilled which foretold that he should follow Tarquin as ruler at Rome.

V

The War with Lars Porsena.

TARQUIN THE PROUD was not content, however, to see his kingdom slip from him so easily; and the Roman people were soon obliged to fight for the right of governing themselves. Their first trouble came from within the city itself; and this, perhaps, no one had expected.

There were some of the people of Rome who were not pleased at the driving away of the king, and who would have been glad to have him back with them again. These persons were young men of high family and much wealth, who had been the companions of the young princes, and who had enjoyed rights and privileges under the rule of Tarquin, which were now taken away from them. They complained bitterly of this, and said that, though the rest of the people had gained by having Tarquin go, they had lost by it. So, when the chance offered itself, they selfishly began to work to bring Tarquin back.

The chance came when Tarquin sent men back to Rome to claim the property which he and his sons had left behind them in the city, when they had been driven away. While these men were in Rome, they secretly made a plot with the dissatisfied young nobles to place King Tarquin on his throne once more. This was treason on the part of the young nobles; but they cared more for their own pleasures than they did for their city. However, the plot was discovered by a slave. From him the consuls learned of it; and they ordered that the plotters should all be seized. Then it was found that among these young men were the two sons of the consul Brutus himself.

This made it very hard for Brutus, for it was part of his duty as consul to act as judge in the trial of prisoners. But he was a true Roman, and loved his country even more than he did his own sons. He took his seat with the other consul, and, when the young men were led before the judges, Brutus did not hesitate to condemn them all to death. Then the prisoners were given into charge of attendants of the consuls, called lictors. The lictors each carried a battle-ax, bound into a bundle of rods, as a sign that the consuls had the right to punish both with the rods and with the ax. They took the young nobles, and first whipped them with the rods, and then put them to death. And the Romans saw, with admiration and pity, that the stern virtue of Brutus did not fail him even when his own sons were put to death before his eyes.

Tarquin was only made more angry and determined by the failure of this plot. He now decided that if he could not get back his throne by a trick, he would try to do so by war. He went about from city to city, begging help from the enemies of Rome to bring that city back under his rule once more. And no matter how often he was refused, or how often when he got help he was defeated in battle, he was always ready to begin again.

At last, Tarquin got the help of a powerful king who

ruled over a part of Tuscany, as the district is called which lies north and west of the Tiber. A fine poem*

LICTORS.

has been written about this war by an English writer, and in it you may read how

*See Macaulay's *Lays of Ancient Rome*.

> Lars Porsena of Clusium,
>   By the Nine Gods he swore
> That the great house of Tarquin
>   Should suffer wrong no more.
> By the Nine Gods he swore it,
>   And named a trysting day,
> And bade his messengers ride forth,
> East and west and south and north,
>   To summon his array.

When the Romans heard this news, they were filled with dismay; and from all sides the country people flocked into the city. Never before had so great a danger threatened that place. But the Senate and consuls prepared as well as they could to meet the attack, and tried to hope that they might still be able to defeat their enemies.

Just across the river from Rome was a long, high hill. Here the Romans had built a fort as a protection to the city; and to connect this with Rome, a wooden bridge had long ago been placed across the rapid stream of the Tiber.

If the Romans could hold this height and the bridge, the city would be safe. But by a quick march, and a fierce attack, the enemies of Rome seized the height. Then they rushed on to gain the bridge also; and many of the Romans who were guarding it were struck with fear, and turned to flee into the city.

At this moment a Roman named Horatius rushed in among those who were fleeing, and sought to stay their flight.

"What good will it do you to flee?" he cried. "If you give up the bridge it will not be long before there are more of the enemy in Rome itself than there are here. Break down the bridge before you go' Meanwhile, I will guard the entrance, so far as one man may."

At these words, the soldiers were seized with shame. While two of their number stepped up to Horatius's side, to defend with him the narrow entrance, the others fell to work with swords and axes and levers to tear down the bridge behind them. When the last timbers were just ready to fall, the soldiers called to Horatius and his brave companions to come back, while there was yet time to cross. His two companions darted back across the swaying timbers; but Horatius lingered to the last. Then, just as he turned to cross, with a mighty crash the bridge fell, and he was left alone with his enemies.

>   Alone stood brave Horatius,
>   But constant still in mind;
>   Thrice thirty thousand foes before,
>   And the broad flood behind.
>   "Down with him!" cried false Sextus,
>   With a smile on his pale face.
>   "Now yield thee," cried Lars Porsena;
>   "Now yield thee to our grace."
>
>   Round turned he, as not deigning
>   Those craven ranks to see;
>   Naught spake he to Lars Porsena,
>   To Sextus naught spake he;
>   But he saw on Palatinus
>   The white porch of his home;
>   And he spake to the noble river
>   That rolls by the towers of Rome.

"O Tiber! Father Tiber!
  To whom the Romans pray,
A Roman's life, a Roman's arms,
  Take thou in charge this day."
So he spake, and speaking sheathed
  The good sword by his side,
And with his harness on his back,
  Plunged headlong in the tide.

No sound of joy or sorrow
  Was heard from either bank;
But friends and foes in dumb surprise
With parted lips and straining eyes,
  Stood gazing where he sank;
And when above the surges
  They saw his crest appear,
All Rome sent forth a rapturous cry,
And even the ranks of Tuscany
  Could scarce forbear to cheer.

But Horatius was weary and wounded from the fight, and his armor weighed heavily upon him. Many times he seemed sinking in midstream, but each time he rose again. At last, he felt the bottom under his feet, and safely climbed the other shore.

The city was saved, and it was mainly Horatius who had saved it. The state was grateful to him for his brave deed. The Senate ordered that he should have as much of the public land as he could plough around in one day; and his statue was set up in the Forum, or market-place, of Rome. But best of all was the gratitude which the citizens, of their own accord, showed him. When food became scarce because of the war with Lars Porsena, the citizens each brought to the house of Horatius little gifts of grain and wine, so that whatever suffering might come upon themselves, there would still be plenty in the house of the man who had saved Rome. And long afterwards we can imagine Roman fathers telling the story to their children:

> When the goodman mends his armor,
>   And trims his helmet's plume;
> When the goodwife's shuttle merrily
>   Goes flashing through the loom;
> With weeping and with laughter
>   Still is the story told,
> How well Horatius kept the bridge
>   In the brave days of old.

VI

The Stories of Mucius and Clœlia.

AFTER Lars Porsena had failed in his attempt to seize the bridge over the Tiber, his army lay for a long time about Rome, and within the city food became very scarce and high in price. Lars Porsena thought that he could starve the city into surrendering, and at last it began to look as though he might succeed. But a young noble named Mucius thought it a disgrace for the Romans to be obliged to lie within the walls, surrounded by the army of the enemy, and to do nothing to help themselves. So he went before the Senate and said:

"O Fathers! permit me to cross the Tiber and attempt to enter the enemy's camp. For it is in my mind to do a great deed, if the gods assist me."

Though they did not know what he planned, the Senate gave him leave to go; and, with a sword concealed under his garment, Mucius set out. When he reached the camp of Lars Porsena, he found a great crowd of soldiers receiving their pay from a man in a purple robe who sat upon a throne. Mucius thought that surely this man must be King Porsena; so he entered the crowd, and, when he had come near enough, he fell upon him and slew him. But this man was only the king's clerk, and the soldiers near by seized Mucius and brought him before the real king for judgment.

When Lars Porsena demanded of the youth who he was and what was the meaning of his deed, Mucius answered:

"Know, O King, that I am a Roman citizen. Mucius is my name. You are the enemy of my country, and I sought to kill you. I know that I shall suffer death, and I have the firmness to meet it. But do you prepare yourself to battle for your life every hour; to have the sword of the enemy at the very entrance of your tent. That is the war which we, the Roman youth, declare against you."

At these words the king was much disturbed, and demanded to know more, and ordered fires to be kindled around the prisoner, if he did not explain the plot which seemed to be formed against him. But Mucius only replied:

"Behold! and see of how little account the body is to those who have great ends in view."

As he said this, he thrust his hand into the fire which was burning upon an altar near by, and held it there without a sign of pain or flinching.

The king, astonished at this act, arose from his throne and commanded that the young man be taken away from the altar. Then the king said to him:

"You have acted more like an enemy to yourself than to me. I should encourage you to be always so brave, if that bravery were only shown upon the side of my country. At all events, I shall now send you back to Rome, untouched and unharmed by me."

Then Mucius replied, as though making a return for the kindness shown him:

"Since bravery is so honored by you, O King, I will

tell you that three hundred of the best of the Roman youth have plotted to attack you in this manner. It was my lot to come first. The rest will follow, each in his turn, until we shall make an end of you."

When Lars Porsena heard this, he saw how hard it would be for him to take Rome, if its people were willing to give up their lives in this way for the city. He sent Mucius back to Rome in safety, where he was honored ever afterwards by the name of the "lefthanded," because his right hand had been destroyed in the altar fire.

Then Porsena agreed to make peace with the Romans, and to take his army away from around the walls of the city. But first he demanded pledges from the Romans that they would keep the peace; and they gave him the sons and daughters of the noblest Roman families, and Lars Porsena took them away with him as hostages, so that he might punish them if the Romans broke the peace.

Among the hostages who were obliged to go with Lars Porsena was a high-spirited girl named Clœlia. She did not like to live as a captive in a strange camp, and she made a plan to escape. Porsena's army then lay not very far from Rome, on the banks of the Tiber; and one day Clœlia, taking a number of other girls with her, managed to swim across the river, and reached Rome in safety.

When the king was told of the escape of the hostages, he was very angry, and sent messengers to Rome to demand that Clœlia and her companions should be sent back to him. The Romans kept their faith, and returned the girls to Porsena; for they thought that they had no right to keep the children simply because they escaped so bravely. When Porsena saw that the Romans were acting fairly in the matter, his anger faded, and he became as generous as they had been just. He led all the Roman prisoners before Clœlia, and bade her choose half of them to return with her to their homes. She chose the youngest among them, and they were then sent back to Rome with great honor, for Lars Porsena said:

"The girl Clœlia is as brave as Mucius and Horatius."

Even after Lars Porsena had made peace with the Romans, Tarquin was not yet satisfied that he would never again be allowed to rule at Rome. When he found that Porsena would no longer help him, he did not rest till he had found another king to fight for him. Then he marched again against Rome, with the armies of thirty cities at his back. The Romans heard with terror of the approach of this great force, for they feared that they would not be able to beat back so many enemies; and to meet their danger, they made a change in their government.

They had found that sometimes the two consuls could not agree, and that the state was weakened by their quarrels. So, in order to prevent this from happening now, while their freedom was to be fought for again, they determined to try another plan. They elected one man to fill the place of a king while the danger lasted, and they called him a Dictator. Every one was to obey him, as though he were a king in truth; and when he led the army out to fight against King Tarquin and his friends once more, the people hoped that they would win the victory.

For a time, however, it seemed that they would be defeated. The soldiers fought bravely, and the Dictator made every effort to win the battle, but at last the men began to give way. Then the Dictator prayed to the twin gods, Castor and Pollux, and vowed to build a temple to them in Rome if they would give their help. Even as he prayed, two youths, on horses as white as snow, rode to the front of the Roman army, and began to press the enemy back, and at last drove them to their camp. But when the Romans had gained their victory, and turned to look for the youths who had saved the day for them, they could find no sign of them except a hoof-print in the rock, such as no earthly horse could have made.

When the army returned to Rome, however, the old men and women, who had been left in the city, told them a wonderful tale. While they had waited in the Forum, for news of the army, two strangers on white horses covered with the foam of battle, had suddenly appeared and ridden to the pool of water by the temple of Vesta. There they had dismounted and bathed their weary horses in the cool water, while they told the people of the victory of Rome. When one of the men who had gathered about them doubted the report which they brought—for it seemed too good to be true, —the youths had smiled and gently touched his beard with their hands; and the hair, which before had been as black as coal, became yellow, like bronze. Then all had believed the good news; and after that the youths mounted again and had ridden away, to be seen no more.

When the Dictator heard this story, he could no

longer doubt that his prayer had been heard. The two youths who had aided the army, and who had brought the news of the victory to Rome, he now knew to be Castor and Pollux. So a temple was built to the twin gods on the spot where they had washed their horses; and some of its columns stand in Rome to this day.

After this battle, Tarquin the Proud was unable to get any one to help him make war on Rome. Two years later he died, and after that there were no more attempts to restore the rule of the Tarquins in the City of the Seven Hills.

VII

Secession of the Plebeians.

DURING all the long years after the founding of the city, Rome had been growing steadily, in spite of her many wars with her enemies. It was not only that her boys and girls grew up to be men and women with children of their own, and in this way the number of people in the city was increased; many persons came to Rome from other places and settled there. Sometimes they did this because the river Tiber made Rome a good place to carry on trade; sometimes they came because the hills of Rome made the city a strong place, where they could be safe from robbers. Sometimes, too, the Romans would conquer the people of another city in battle, and would bring them in a body to live at Rome. So, in many ways, the number of the people in the city grew, until it was said that, about the time that King Tarquin was driven out, there were as many as eighty thousand men in Rome, who could serve in war if there was need of them.

This was a good thing for Rome in some ways, but in one way it was bad. The new people and their children were not allowed to take part in the government, so the Romans came to be divided into two classes. The descendants of the old families were called patricians, and they alone could hold the offices and be priests. **The descendants** of the new-comers were called plebeians; **and,** though they could own property, and carry on business, and sometimes were allowed to vote, yet they could not be elected to any office and in other ways were not allowed the full rights of Roman citizens.

After King Tarquin was driven away **from** the city, **the** plebeians became worse off than they had been before. The patrician consuls and the patrician Senate used their power for the good of their own class. The patricians alone were allowed to use **the** public land,—from which, you will remember, some was given **to Horatius as a reward.** But worst of all **was the cruel law of** debt, which **was** now enforced against the plebeians more harshly than ever before.

When a poor plebeian returned from fighting **in the** wars of his country, he might find that the crops on his little farm outside of Rome had been destroyed by the enemy, and his cattle had been driven off. Then he would be obliged **to** borrow money **of** some rich patrician to help pay his taxes and support his family until **the** next harvest could be gathered. But, if another war followed during the **next** summer, he would have to leave **his farm** again, and so could not pay his debt when he had promised. Then he might be seized and put into prison, and even sold as a slave, by the man to whom **he** owed the money.

In this way, **many** plebeians suffered from the harsh laws, and they became **very** much discontented. **At** last, one day, an old soldier appeared **in** the marketplace **at** Rome, appealing to the people in his great misery. His clothes were soiled and torn, and his hair and beard had grown long and shaggy over his pale, thin face. But in spite of his pitiful appearance he was recognized as a man who had been a brave officer in the army, and on his body could be seen many scars which he had gained in battle.

"While I have been fighting in your wars," he cried, "the enemy have destroyed the crops upon my land; they have burned my house and driven off my cattle. The money which I was compelled to borrow, I could not pay back. So my farm has been taken from me; I have been thrown into prison; and see! here are the marks of the whip upon my back."

When the people heard his story and saw his wretched condition, a great tumult arose. The people rushed upon the houses of the patricians and set free the prisoners whom they found in them. Soon, from every side, men came running who had suffered like this brave man from the cruel laws of debt; and the market-place was filled with angry shouts.

In the midst of this trouble news came that their enemies, the Volscians, were on the march toward Rome. At first the plebeians refused to enlist in the army, which was called to go out to fight them. When they were promised, however, that the laws about debts should be changed, they gave in their names and marched out to the war. Then, when the Volscians had been defeated, and the war was over, the patricians refused to change the laws as they had promised. After a great deal of trouble, the plebeians at last determined to settle the matter for themselves. You have read that the Romans learned two things under their kings,—to fight and to obey. They believed that they must obey their laws and their rulers even if they were cruel and unjust; and, although they were now greatly abused, they did not use their arms against the men who ruled them. Instead of killing and burning, the plebeians formed another plan.

"We cannot use force against our consuls," they said, "but we will leave the patricians to fight for themselves when the next army comes marching against the city. We will let them receive the wounds and bear the evils from which we have been suffering."

Then they marched out from the city, and set up an armed camp on the Sacred Mount, which was not far from Rome. There they waited quietly for many days, without attacking any one and taking only enough food from the people of the country to keep themselves from starving.

Meanwhile, in Rome the consuls and the Senate were filled with dismay. The main support of the state was gone, and the patricians began to realize how much they had depended upon the plebeians for the good of the city. There was nothing now to stand between them and an enemy, and they trembled to think what would become of Rome if an army should now come marching against it. When they heard that the men upon the Sacred Mount were talking of beginning a new city, as Romulus and his companions had done, they felt that they must give way, or else sacrifice themselves and their city. At last, they sent a man to the people to offer to make terms with them. He was a wise and eloquent man, and he had been chosen because he was beloved by the common people. The plebeians admitted him willingly to their camp, and listened eagerly to his message. He began by telling them a story.

"Once upon a time," he said, "the other parts of the human body began to grumble because they had all the work to do, while the stomach lay idle in their midst, and enjoyed the results of their labors. So they agreed that the hands should not carry food to the mouth, or the mouth receive it, or the teeth chew it. In this way, they thought to starve the stomach into submission. But soon they found that the different members, and even the entire body itself, began to grow weak and thin, and that, the more they starved the stomach, the weaker they all became. Then they began to see that the service of the stomach was by no means a small one; that it not only received nourishment, but supplied it to all the parts, and that the members of the body could not themselves live and do their work without it."

As you can easily see, the messenger meant to show the people, by this fable, that the inhabitants of a city form one great body, with each class depending upon every other for its welfare. The people listened patiently to him, and saw the truth in what he said. In the end, they returned to Rome, but only after the patricians had agreed that, from this time on, the plebeians should have a number of officers of their own, called Tribunes, to protect them.

These tribunes were given very high powers. When anything was being done, even if it were by the consuls themselves, the tribunes could step forth and say, "Veto!" which means, "I forbid it!" and at once it must stop. No one might harm a tribune in any way, and during the year that they held office, the tribunes always slept in their own houses in the city, with their doors open day and night, so that no one might seek their aid in vain.

With the tribunes to help them in their difficulties, the common people were relieved of many of their troubles. But still the struggle between the patricians and the plebeians lasted for nearly two hundred years longer, and did not cease until the plebeians had been given equal rights in the government with the patricians. Through all this long struggle there was very little bloodshed, and there was never war between the two classes. And often, when the struggle was at its fiercest, the patricians and plebeians would lay aside their quarrels, and march out, side by side, to fight the enemies of their city.

In this way the Romans learned something better than how to fight battles successfully,—they learned how to govern themselves. The patricians always held out for their rights just as long as they could, but when they were beaten, they knew how to give way and make the best of it. From these struggles the whole people learned obedience and self-control, and so became fit to rule themselves, and other lands also, when they grew strong enough to conquer them.

VIII

The Story of Coriolanus.

NOT long after the people had gained their tribunes to protect them, a noble lady, named Veturia, lived in Rome. She was a widow, and had but one son, Caius Marcius, whom she loved very dearly. From his babyhood, Caius was a strong, brave boy, and his mother had every reason to be proud of him, except for one fault. He had a violent temper, and never learned to control it; and, in the end, this brought great trouble upon both his mother and himself.

Caius was proud of his mother, and proud of belonging to the noblest class in the city; and from his earliest youth, he tried to make himself worthy of both. At that time, almost the only training of a Roman youth was for war, and the stories say that Caius labored so faithfully to learn the use of weapons, and to make his body strong, that there was soon no youth in the city who could equal him.

At last, the time came when Caius Marcius went to his first battle, and in this he proved himself to be a good fighter, although he was still almost a boy. He came back to his mother with a crown of oak leaves upon his head, which was the way in which the Romans honored those of their soldiers who had not only fought bravely in battle, but who had also succeeded in saving the life of a Roman citizen.

You may be sure that the heart of the lady Veturia was glad and proud, when she saw her son riding home to her from his first battle, with the wreath of honor upon his brow. But she had still greater cause to rejoice later, for, as time went on, and Caius was called to fight for his city again and again, she never once saw him return without honors and rewards. And his greatest pleasure in his honors was the pride and delight which his mother took in them.

At one time, when Marcius was fighting with the Roman army, they were besieging the city of Corioli, in the country of the Volscians. As the soldiers lay camped about the city, they heard that a large force was marching to attack them from behind. The consul, who was leading the Romans, did not wish to be caught between the walls of Corioli and a fresh army, and thus be attacked on both sides at once. So he divided the army into two parts, and left the smaller part to watch the town, while he marched against the army of the Volscians with the other.

When the people of Corioli saw that only a small part of the Roman army was left to lay siege to their city, they came rushing out from their gates to attack them. The Romans were driven back, and they would have been defeated if it had not been for Marcius. So fiercely did he attack the enemy that they were forced to give way before him. Then he encouraged his companions to pursue the flying soldiers to their city gates. Even there he was not willing to stop, but, still urging his men onward, he rushed into Corioli after the defeated enemy, and kept them at bay, and the gates open, until the rest of the army could come up and take the city.

Then, as though he had done nothing to give him need of rest, he led a part of the men to help the consul in his fight against the Volscians. They arrived just as the battle was beginning, and fought bravely with the others until the victory was won. After the battle was over, Marcius was offered much rich booty as a reward, but this he would not take. He accepted only the horse of the consul, which was pressed upon him as a gift, and asked but one favor.

"I have one request to make," he said, "and this I hope you will not deny me. There is a friend of mine among the Volscian prisoners, a man of virtue, who has often entertained me at his house. He has lost his wealth and his freedom, and is now to be sold as a common slave. Let me beg that this may not be done, and that I may be allowed to save him from this last misfortune."

The consul granted this request, and Marcius returned to Rome with no other reward than this for his brave deed. But, in honor of what he had done, the people gave him a third name, which was formed from that of the city which he had taken; and, after this, he was called Caius Marcius Coriolanus. His mother, who was as proud as Coriolanus himself, must have been better pleased with this title for her son than if he had brought home a great treasure to enrich the family.

If Coriolanus could have been always with the army, doing such brave deeds, the rest of his story might have been very different. But, as he was a Roman patrician, he was not only a soldier, but one of the rulers of the city as well. The proud, fierce temper, which Marcius had shown even in his boyhood, began to exhibit itself more and more plainly as he grew to be an older man and took more part in the affairs of the city.

He thought that only the patricians should have part in the government of Rome, and he hated the tribunes, who could stop the patrician consuls by their veto. This made the plebeians fear him, and, though the nobles admired him for his courage, and wished to make him consul, the people refused to elect him. Marcius was bitterly angry over this defeat, and was never willing to forget that he had been so slighted after his services to the city.

Then a time came when the dislike which Coriolanus had for the plebeians made him do an unwise thing, which proved to be his ruin.

On account of the many wars which had laid waste the fields, there was not enough grain raised on the lands of Rome to feed her people; and the consuls sent even as far as Sicily for corn to keep the city from famine until the next harvest time. When the grain came to Rome, it seemed to bring more trouble than comfort to the starving citizens; for Coriolanus proposed to the Senate that they should not allow the poor people to receive the grain until they had promised to give up their tribunes, and be governed entirely by the patricians, as before. Some of the senators were wise enough to see that this would never do, and when the people arose, and threatened the Senate, it gave way in spite of Coriolanus, and allowed the corn to be sold at a low price.

But the people were not satisfied with receiving their grain. They now so feared and hated Coriolanus, for having tried to starve them into giving up their rights, that they would no longer have him in their city. He was brought to trial by the tribunes, and the people sentenced him to banishment for life from Rome.

Coriolanus went away with his heart full of bitterness. He could not see that he had been wrong, and he felt only hatred now for the Roman people, who, as it seemed to him, had abused and mistreated him. He went, therefore, to the country of the Volscians, against whom he had fought so many battles for the Romans. At the fall of night, he came to the house of one of their chiefs. There he entered and seated himself as a suppliant at the hearth, with his mantle covering his face. He had such an air of pride and sorrow that the members of the family did not dare to question him, but sent for Tullus, the master of the house. Tullus immediately went to him, and asked him who he was and for what purpose he had come to him. Then Coriolanus arose and threw the covering from his head, and looked him proudly in the face.

"Do you not remember me?' he said. "I am that Caius Marcius who has brought so much trouble upon the Volscians. If I were to deny this, my name of Coriolanus would still declare me your enemy. That name is the one thing which I received in reward for my perils and hardships in battles, and it is the one thing that the Romans have left me, as they send me forth an exile. Now I come, an humble suppliant at your hearth, not for protection, but for revenge. Let me lead your people against the Romans, and you will have the advantage of a general who knows all the secrets of your enemies. If I may not do this, let me perish as your foe, for I no longer wish to live."

Tullus was rejoiced to give him what he asked, and soon Coriolanus marched against Rome with a Volscian army at his back. When he came near the city, the Romans were seized with fear, for they felt too weak to contend against the Volscians, when led by Coriolanus.

The senators and the people, therefore, agreed to send messengers to Coriolanus, offering to restore him to his place at Rome, and begging him not to bring the terror and distress of war upon his city. These messengers were chosen from among the friends and relatives of Coriolanus, in order that they might have more influence with him. But he treated them harshly, as if he had altogether forgotten his former love for them, and no peace could be settled upon. Then the Romans sent all the priests of Rome, clothed in their sacred robes, to beg for peace; but they also were turned away.

Then the city was given over to despair, for the people felt that there was no cruelty of the harshest enemy that could be compared with the fierce wrath of the exiled Coriolanus. The old men knelt weeping at the altars of the gods, and the women ran wailing through the streets of the city. But Veturia, the mother of Coriolanus, gathered about her the wife of her son, his children, and the noblest women of the town, and set out for the camp of the Volscians to try what she could do.

Coriolanus saw the company of Roman women moving as suppliants through his camp, but he watched them unmoved, until he recognized his mother at their head. Then his proud soul was shaken, and he ran to her with his arms outstretched, as though he were the little Caius once more. But his mother drew back and spoke sternly and sadly to him.

"Do I behold you, my son," she cried, "in arms against the walls of Rome? Tell me, before I receive your embrace, whether I am in your camp as a captive or as your mother. Does length of life give me only this, to behold my son an exile and an enemy? If I had not been a mother, Rome would not have been besieged! If I had not had a son, I might die free, in a free country! But be sure of this, my son, that you shall not be able to reach your country to harm it, unless you first cross the body of your mother."

As Veturia spoke these words, she threw herself down upon the ground at the feet of Coriolanus, as a suppliant before her own son. But Marcius, weeping, raised her from the earth, and cried:

"O Mother! what is this that you have done to me! You have saved Rome, but destroyed your son. I go, conquered by you alone."

Then Coriolanus led his army away from Rome; and it is said that he met his death at the hands of the disappointed Volscians. Veturia returned in loneliness to Rome, mourning for her beloved son; but she held him less dear than she did her country's freedom.

IX

The Family of the Fabii.*

THE family of the Fabii, and, indeed, all the families of Rome, were very different from our own American families, or any others that you may know about. You think of your family as being made up of your father and mother, brothers and sisters, and, it may be, a grandfather or a grandmother who lives with you. You have other relatives, of course,—aunts, uncles, and cousins; but perhaps these live far away in some other part of the country, and you may know very little about them. Even if you have a family of cousins living in the same town with you, you do not think of them as belonging to your own family, as your brothers and sisters do.

This was all very different in the city of Rome. There the families were held closer together than with us, and cousins that were so distantly related that we should scarcely think them cousins at all, were all counted in the great family to which their fathers and grandfathers and great-grandfathers had belonged for centuries before them. This made the families very

---

*Many Latin words ended in the letters "us" in the singular number. To make the plural of such words, the "us" was changed to "i." In this way, the name "Fabius," in the singular number, becomes "Fabii" when we wish to speak of more than one person.

THE FAMILY OF THE FABII.

large,—as large, perhaps, as your own would be if you could go back through all your grandfathers to the first one who came to America, and then should gather together all the persons in the country to-day who are related to him, however distantly.

If you will only think for a moment of how many this might be, you will not be surprised to find that the family of the Fabii, counting men, women and children, is supposed to have contained many hundreds of persons. Of course, all these people did not live in the same house, as we think of families doing to-day, for that would have been impossible. But they all bore the name of Fabius, and they all obeyed the head of their family more readily than sons nowadays obey their own fathers.

The Fabii belonged to the patrician class, and were richer and more powerful than any other family in Rome; so, year after year, some one of them was sure to be elected consul. At last, the common people grew weary of this, especially as the Fabii always opposed the tribunes in everything that they wished to do for the good of the people. The plebeians grew to dislike the Fabii so much that they were willing to do anything to distress and annoy them.

While the people were in this humor, Kæso Fabius, who was then one of the consuls, led the Roman army against the enemy. He left the city with his horsemen and foot soldiers, and drew up his men before the enemy's camp. He was a good general, and everything was well arranged for the battle, when he gave the signal for the attack; but, at the command, the cavalry alone, who were all patricians or rich men, obeyed and went against the foe. The plebeians, who were the foot soldiers, hated their consuls so much that they stood still and refused to go forward and take their part in the battle. They did this, not because they were afraid to fight, but because they wished to see their consul go back to Rome disgraced by defeat.

Though the Fabii were proud and haughty men, they now saw that they had gone too far in their harshness toward the common people.

When some of Rome's neighbors heard of this trouble at Rome, they agreed that this would be a good time to lead their forces against the city and make an end of the Romans altogether. So, during the next year, another force, from several cities, came marching together against Rome.

The Roman Senate was greatly distressed at this, for one of the consuls was again a Fabius, and they had no way of making sure that the soldiers would not behave in the same way that they had done the year before. Indeed, the soldiers left home with a sullen look, as though they were determined to show their anger again, even at the risk of bringing ruin upon the city. For this reason, the consuls were afraid to trust their men in battle, and when they came near the enemy, they pitched their camp, and fortified it, and quietly kept their soldiers within it.

Day by day, and week by week, the army lay within its camp. The enemies of the Romans now began to think that there was trouble again between the patricians and the people, and that the soldiers had again refused to fight. They were delighted at this, and felt as though the victory was already won. Often they would come close to the Roman camp and scoff at the soldiers who lay within.

"You pretend to disagree," they would call, mockingly, "so that you may not show how afraid of us you are. Your consuls fear to lead you to battle, for they distrust your courage even more than your obedience."

The Romans could not endure these insults for very long. Soon, the men who had come out of Rome determined not to fight, were begging their consuls to lead them against the enemy. But Fabius did not think that they were ready yet; so he only replied:

"The time has not yet come."

The soldiers were still forced to remain closely in their camp, and listen yet longer to the taunting cries of the enemy, who called "Cowards, cowards," and, at last, threatened to attack the camp itself. Then, when Fabius saw that the Romans could no longer be kept from attacking the enemy who insulted them, he drew the army up and said to them:

"Soldiers, I know that you are able to conquer these men who mock you; but what makes me hesitate to give battle is the doubt whether you will do it, or will stand still in the face of the enemy, as you did last year. I have, therefore, determined not to give the signal for battle until you will swear by the gods that you will return victorious. Our soldiers have once deceived the Roman consuls; the gods they will never deceive."

Then one of the foremost soldiers raised his hand and cried:

"Fabius, I will return victorious from the field or die upon it. If I deceive you, may the anger of Jupiter, Mars, and all the gods be upon me."

Following his example, the whole army took the same oaths. They were then led forth to battle, and, after a hard fight, during which the soldiers were faithful to the last, they defeated the enemy.

After this, the Fabian family tried rather to favor the poorer people than to be harsh and stern in their treatment of them. Kæso Fabius ordered all the soldiers who were wounded in this battle to be cared for in the houses of the rich; and in the homes of the Fabii, these men were treated more kindly than anywhere else. In this way, little by little, the people forgot their hatred of the Fabii, and began to look upon them as their friends. And the Fabii soon proved that, however proud they might be, they were willing to give everything for the safety of their city.

There came a time when all the enemies of Rome seemed to be taking up arms against her at once, and the people were over-burdened with the preparations for meeting so many enemies, in so many different directions. As the Senate was anxiously discussing the means of meeting the danger, Kæso Fabius arose, and, speaking for all the Fabian family, he said:

"Fathers, do you attend to the other wars. Appoint the Fabii as the enemies of the Veientians. We pledge ourselves that the honor of the Roman name shall be safe in that quarter. And, as we ask this war for our family, it is our plan to conduct it at our own expense. For the city, which is so burdened with other dangers, should be spared the expense of soldiers and of supplies in this direction."

The Senate accepted this offer with joy and thankfulness, and the next day the Fabii left the town.

There were three hundred and six men, all patricians and all Fabii, in this little army. The people, quite forgetting their former dislike of the family, followed them through the streets of the city; and, at the altar of each god, they begged that the brave men might go forth to victory, and return safely to their homes once more.

These prayers, however, were all in vain. No one of that little company ever came back to Rome. They went forth and built a fort facing the lands of their enemies, and they kept them in check for many months. But at last they were surprised and overcome by them, and all of the army of the Fabii were killed.

Only one boy, who had been too young to go with his relatives, remained of that great family of brave men. But this boy became, in time, the head of another Fabian family, which was to win as much honor at Rome as the one that had been destroyed.

X

The Victory of Cincinnatus.

ON the slopes of the mountains east of Rome, there lived a sturdy people called the Æquians. The Romans had to struggle with this people for many years after the driving out of their kings. As soon as one war with them was ended, another was sure to begin; and it was during one of these wars that a Roman named Cincinnatus made his name so famous that the Roman people loved to tell his story as long as their city lasted.

It happened once that a band of these Æquians marched into the Roman lands, and began to burn and plunder on every side. Now, a treaty of peace had been made between the Romans and the Æquians just the year before; so the Senate sent messengers to the intruders, to complain of their conduct.

When the messengers reached the camp of the Æquians, they found the chiefs of the band sitting in the shade of a great oak tree.

"Why do you come into our lands," the messengers asked, "making war in time of peace, and breaking the treaty which you have made with us? The Roman Senate demands that you make a return for what you have destroyed, and leave the country in peace."

The leader of the Æquians would hear no more than this.

"The Roman Senate!" he exclaimed in scorn. "Deliver to this oak tree whatever instructions you have brought from the Roman Senate, and in the meantime, I will attend to other matters!" And he turned away to leave them.

Then the Roman messengers also prepared to depart, for they saw that nothing could be done in the way of a peaceful settlement. But, as they turned to go, one of them cried:

"Let both this sacred oak and all the gods be witnesses that the treaty is broken by you; and so may they help our arms presently, when we shall seek to avenge ourselves."

Then they went away, and soon a Roman consul led an army against the Æquians. This consul was not a brave and ready man, as most of the Romans were, and the Æquians soon discovered that he was afraid to come to battle with them. Then they laid siege to his camp, and by throwing up earthworks around it, they had the army safe as if in a trap. Five of the Romans, however, succeeded in passing through the lines of the enemy, and hurried to the city with the news that the army was surrounded.

When the Romans heard this news, they were struck with dismay. The Senate was hurriedly called together, and they decided that a Dictator must be appointed; and Lucius Quintius, who was called "Cincinnatus," on account of his crisp, curly hair, was the one whom they chose for that office.

Cincinnatus, though he was a good soldier and a patrician, was a poor man, and tilled his own little farm of four acres on the other side of the River Tiber.

When the messengers of the Senate came, early in the morning, to announce to him that he had been appointed Dictator, they found him ploughing in the fields without his "toga," or gown. Before telling him their business, they bade him leave his work, and put on his toga, that he might listen with due respect to the commands of the Senate.

At this, Cincinnatus was astonished, and, asking frequently whether anything was the matter, he

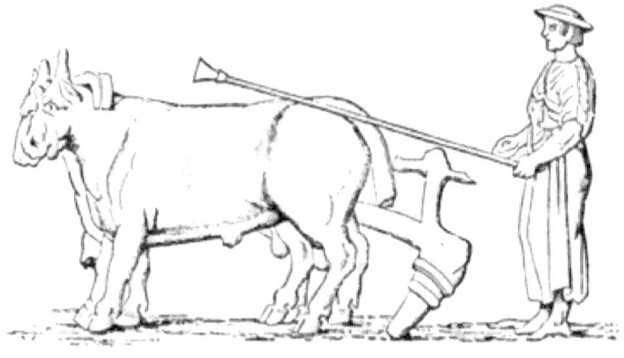

ROMAN PLOUGH.

bade his wife bring his toga from his cottage. Then washing himself free from the dust and sweat of his work, he wrapped himself in his gown, as though he were in the Senate house, and listened to the messengers.

They saluted him as Dictator, and, explaining the terror that ruled in the city, they bade him come to Rome and take the command. Cincinnatus obeyed, and went with them to the city, where he was met at the gates by his sons; and with twenty-four lictors marching on before him, he was escorted to his house in the city

When the next day dawned, Cincinnatus went into the assembly of the people, and commanded all business to be stopped, and forbade any one from attending to his own affairs. Then he commanded that all who were of the age to act as soldiers should come together in the Field of Mars before sunset, with their arms, and with food for five days; and he ordered that each should bring with him twelve large wooden stakes. Those who were too old to act as soldiers he ordered to prepare the food for the other men, while these were busy cutting the stakes.

When the appointed time came, the men set out, with Cincinnatus marching before them, and bidding them hasten.

"The consul and his army have now been besieged three days," he said. "It is uncertain what each day and night may bring with it. You must hasten, that we may reach the camp this very night, for often the gain of a moment will change defeat into victory."

And the men, to please their leader and encourage themselves, called to one another:

"Follow, soldiers! Hasten on!"

At midnight they reached the camp, where the Æquians were laying siege to the Romans. Cincinnatus first rode all around the place in order to discover, as well as he could in the darkness, how it was arranged. Then he drew his men silently in a long column around the camp, and directed that when the signal should be given, they should all raise a shout, and begin digging a trench and driving their stakes before it for defense.

When all was ready, the signal was given; and their

shout rose through the silent night, terrifying the Æquians, and carrying joy to the hearts of the imprisoned consul and his army. These sprang to their feet, crying:

"That is the shout of our countrymen! Help is at hand! Let us also attack the enemy!"

Then the imprisoned Romans seized their arms, and rushed upon the Æquians just as they were turning to attack the soldiers of Cincinnatus. It was scarcely daylight before the Romans had conquered; for the Æquians were attacked from both sides at once, and were fighting unknown numbers in the darkness of the night.

After the battle was over, the enemies of the Romans were not destroyed, for Cincinnatus said:

"I want not the blood of the Æquians. Let them depart in peace. But, before they go, we must have a confession that their nation is defeated and subdued. They must all pass under the yoke."

Then he ordered two spears to be driven into the earth, and a third one fastened across their tops; and under this all the Æqui were obliged to pass, without their arms, and with but one garment on their backs. This was meant to show to all the world that the Æquians were now as peaceful and subdued as the patient oxen that ploughed the Roman fields with the yoke upon their necks.

Cincinnatus then prepared to return to Rome at once. He gave all the booty of the camp of the Æquians to his own soldiers, and punished the consul for his cowardice by giving him and his soldiers nothing.

When they reached the city, they found it full of joy at the rescue of its army. The Senate voted that Cincinnatus should enter Rome in triumph. So he marched into the city by the "Gate of Triumph," with the chiefs of the Æquians led before him, and the standards of the army carried around his car. The soldiers followed after, loaded down with their booty. Tables, covered with provisions, are said to have been laid out before the houses of all, and the soldiers were fed in abundance, as they followed the car of their general with shouts and rejoicing.

Cincinnatus, however, was not made over-proud by his great victory and by the honor that was shown him afterwards. On the sixteenth day after he had received the command, he laid down his power, and returned to his little farm and his ploughing; and he has been as much admired for this act as for his great success as a general.

At the close of the Revolutionary War, which made our country free from England, Washington and his companions did the same thing which you see Cincinnatus doing so many centuries before them. They gave up their places as generals and officers in the army, and went peacefully back to their farms and shops again. They thought of Cincinnatus at that time, and of how they were following his example; and they joined together and formed a society which they called the "Society of the Cincinnati," after this old Roman. This society, in its turn, gave its name to a city which bears it yet, the city of Cincinnati, in the state of Ohio. From this you can see how long a man's name may last in the world, if he is only strong and noble enough to do something which people will be glad to remember always.

XI

The Laws of the Twelve Tables.

AS you read these tales of Tarquin and Horatius, Coriolanus, and Cincinnatus, you may think, perhaps, that the teaching of King Numa was wasted, and that the Romans after him did nothing but fight, and studied nothing but the art of winning battles. Almost all of the oldest stories that have come down to us tell us only of the defeat or victory of a Roman army,—for that seemed the one important thing to the men who wrote the records. This, however, did not make up all the life of the Roman people. They were something else besides soldiers: they were citizens of Rome, and were members of family groups; and much might have been told us about their life in the city of which we shall always be ignorant.

The wisest men among the Romans at this time knew very little about the world, even as it was then; and they could never have imagined, if they had tried ever so hard, what the boys and girls, who would be living more than two thousand years after they were dead, would like to know about them. They only thought, as they wrote their records, that by the favor of the gods their city should last forever, and that, after many years, their own people might have forgotten when some city was taken, or how some army had been destroyed. So they wrote down these facts, and made them as lasting as they could; and they did not imagine that, after twenty centuries, people would rather know more of how they bought and sold in their market-places, and prayed in their temples, and behaved to one another in their homes, than so much about their little armies, and the towns that they captured, and the fields of their enemies that they laid waste.

The story of the Twelve Tables of the Law, however, is not about battles; and in it you will hear of no consul leading his soldiers out of the city to meet the enemy, and of no Dictator returning in triumph, after winning a victory for his country. It is not a tale of war, but of the beginning of written laws among the Romans, and it is a much nobler story for the Roman people than that of any of their battles.

When we Americans speak of the Law, we think of the laws which are printed in many books, and which are used by our judges and lawyers in trying cases in our courts. The Romans, at first, did not know anything of this kind of law. Such laws as they had were all unwritten, and were only known to the patricians who had handed them down by word of mouth from father to son, for many hundreds of years. The common people did not know them, and they had no way of finding out what was right for them to do, except by asking some one who had been taught the law from his early youth.

This might not have been so hard for the common people if all the patricians had learned the same law, and used their knowledge justly. But there were many different rules about the same thing, and the men who wished to be unfair could choose the law that would be most to their advantage, and of the least help to the people who appealed to them. By this unfair dealing, the people were often misled and treated very unjustly in their dealings with the patricians; but as they did not know the law, and had no way of learning it, they could do nothing to help themselves.

It was one of the tribunes of the people who at last tried to aid them by giving them the knowledge that was lacking to them. He proposed that all the laws of Rome should be gathered together and published, so that the people could understand what they must and must not do, and so avoid making mistakes because of ignorance. The patricians of Rome were opposed to this, for they did not wish the knowledge of the law to be given to the plebeians. They felt that this would be giving up even more of their rights over the people than they had surrendered when the people were brought back from the Sacred Mount and given their tribunes to protect them.

For this reason, the Senate refused to consent to the publishing of the law. But the people had now learned to be as firm in what they demanded as the Senate. Year after year, they elected only those men for tribunes who promised to help them in this struggle; and year after year, the tribunes continued to demand patiently and firmly the publication of the laws. It was ten years, however, before the Senate finally gave up the struggle, and allowed the people to have their own way.

Then they all agreed upon a curious thing. They changed their whole government for the time during which the laws were to be written; and instead of electing consuls and tribunes, as usual, they chose ten men who were both to govern the city and to get the laws ready for the people.

After working together for some time over their task, these men called the people together and said to them:

"We have written the laws as justly toward the highest and the lowest as it can be done by the consideration of ten men. The understanding and advice of a greater number might prove more successful. We bid you, therefore, go and read the laws that are placed before you, and consider them in your own minds in each particular, and talk together concerning them, in order that you may discover everything in which they are at fault. For we wish you to seem not to have accepted the laws proposed for you, but to have proposed them for yourselves."

Then the people did as they were bidden, and when all the faults of the laws seemed to have been corrected, they were approved by the assembly of the people; and they were published so that all men might see them.

But perhaps you will ask: "How could they be published, if there were no printing presses and books among the Romans, such as we have now?"

The Romans used a simple plan, but one that answered very well. They carved their laws upon twelve tablets of bronze, and then hung them in their market-place, or Forum, as they called it, on the sides of the stand where the Romans took their places when they wished to make a speech to the assembly of the people.

Here, in this public place, every man who could read was free to come and study them. As the Forum was the busiest place in Rome, where each citizen came at some time during almost every day of his life in the city, you will see that, after this, they lived with their laws constantly before their eyes. The boys, too, were obliged to learn the Twelve Tables by heart, as part of their education, and we may easily believe that it was not hard for a bright boy, who would be glad for an excuse to linger in the bustling Forum, to learn the whole contents of the tables before he was very old. Certainly, there was no excuse now for the Romans of any class not to know what was lawful and unlawful; and in this way a nobler thing had been done than if the Romans had conquered many cities, and sold their peoples into slavery.

These bronze tablets of the law have not come down to us through the centuries, as some of the Roman buildings have done. They were broken and destroyed long ago; but most of their contents have been preserved for us in the writings of the later Romans. Some of these laws seem very strange to us now, who are living with such different manners and customs; and this, perhaps, is most true of the laws that concern the family.

The father of the Roman family was like a ruler in a little kingdom all his own, in which no one, not even the consul, could interfere. He could do exactly as he pleased with his wife and his children and his servants. His children never grew up and became independent of their father, as you will be of your father when you become of age. The Roman father kept his power over his sons and daughters until the day of his death, and the laws even allowed him to sell his children as slaves, or to hire them out to work for his profit, whether they wished to do so or not.

But, besides the laws which seem to us so strange, there were many which seem much more reasonable. Among these was one which declared that if a tree overhung the ground of a neighbor, the neighbor might take the fruit that dropped on his side of the line. If any one cut down the trees which belonged to another, he must pay twenty-five pounds of copper for each tree. If any one turned cattle into a neighbor's grain field, or cut down his grain by night, he was to be severely punished.

As time went on, some of the laws of the twelve tables were changed among the Romans, and a great many others were added to them. Then it became impossible for any one to learn all of the laws by heart, and at last the boys ceased to learn even the laws of the twelve tables. But the main principles of the Roman law remained the same under every change; the laws were only made clearer, and juster, and better fitted to the changes in the world to which they were to be applied. So the Roman law survived when almost everything else of the Roman rule had passed away, and it is the foundation of the law of many nations of the world to this day.

XII

How Camillus Captured Veii.

ABOUT twenty miles north of Rome was a large and powerful city called Veii, with which the Romans were often at war. It was in a struggle with this city that the Fabii had been destroyed; and after that many other wars followed, until, about a hundred years after the kings were driven from Rome, a struggle began in which the Romans at last conquered their old enemy.

This was the fourteenth war between Rome and Veii. When the Romans had laid siege to the town for eight long years, and it seemed as though they would never be able to conquer it, the Senate and the people all became discouraged. Then a strange thing happened to make them more disturbed.

About as far south of Rome as Veii was north of it, was a lake called the Alban Lake, which was completely surrounded by hills, and had no inlet or outlet for its waters. News now came to Rome that the water of this lake had suddenly begun to rise higher and higher, without any heavy rains, or any other cause that could be discovered. The Romans, therefore, imagined that this was a miracle which was performed by the gods; and to find out the meaning of it, they sent messengers to the Oracle of the god Apollo, at Delphi. But before these messengers had returned, the Romans received an explanation of the matter from the Veientians themselves.

As often happens in long sieges, the soldiers of the two armies had got in the habit of calling back and forth at one another. One day, as they were doing this, an old man stood upon the walls of Veii and declared, like one uttering a prophecy, that "until the waters should be discharged from the Alban Lake, the Romans should never become the masters of Veii."

One of the Roman soldiers caught at this saying eagerly, thinking that perhaps it showed a way for them to become at last victorious. He persuaded the old man to come out from the walls, and talk with him in the open ground before the Roman camp; then, when they were alone, he seized him boldly about the waist, and carried him by main force into the camp. From there he was taken to the Senate at Rome; and here he was ordered to repeat the prophecy which he had spoken upon the walls of his city. He replied:

"The gods were angry with the Veientian people, that day, when they bade me show the way to ruin my country, from the walls of Veii. But, since it seemed to them well for me to speak it, it is better said than unsaid. It is written in the books of the fates that whenever the Alban water shall rise to a great height, and the Romans shall discharge it in the proper manner, victory will be granted to them. Until that is done, the gods will not desert the walls of Veii."

When the Romans found that the answer of the Oracle of Apollo agreed with the statement of the old man, they set eagerly to work to do what was required of them.

While some remained with the army to watch about the walls of Veii, others worked at the Alban Lake. There they cut a great tunnel through the rock of the hills, to make a passage for the imprisoned waters; and the remains of that tunnel can be seen to this day. Then ditches were dug through the country, and the water of the lake was let out upon the fields. This was in obedience to the commands of the Oracle, and by doing this the Romans believed that they prepared the way for the destruction of Veii.

After all this was done, a Roman named Camillus was appointed Dictator, to complete the capture of the city. When he reached the place he withdrew the Romans into their camp, and kept them closely there, in order that there might be no chance for speech with the enemy. Then he began a tunnel which was to lead from the camp, under the walls of the city, and into the very citadel of the town. Day and night his soldiers worked at this, each in his turn, so that no one should become exhausted by the hard labor. At last the work was all completed, except breaking through the last thin wall of earth, which would admit them into the city.

The Veientians still laughed and shouted from their walls at the silent Romans, all unconscious that the Alban Lake had disappeared into the earth, and that their enemies were ready to pour into the city from their tunnel. But Camillus was certain of his victory, and having given orders for the soldiers to take their arms, he went forth to beg the help and favor of the gods.

"Under thy guidance, O Apollo," he prayed, "I proceed to destroy the city of Veii, and I vow to thee a tenth part of the spoil."

Then some of the Romans attacked the walls. As the Veientians rushed to their defense, others of the Romans came out of the tunnel in the city and attacked them from behind. The Veientians were taken by surprise, and the Romans who were in the city soon succeeded in opening the gates of the town for their companions. In this way, the Romans soon won a complete victory. When the battle was over, the people of Veii were made slaves, and the town was stripped of all its treasures by the soldiers who had conquered it.

Then the Romans prepared to remove the gods also from the captured city. A band of young men was chosen, and, with their bodies freshly washed in pure water, and clad in white garments, they took their way in a solemn procession to the temple of the great Juno. She was the especial god of the Veientians, and they entered her temple with fear and awe. When they stood before the image of the goddess, one of the company asked:

"O Juno, art thou willing to go to Rome?"

The Romans believed that they saw the goddess bow her beautiful head in assent; and they all shouted with joy at this favorable response. Then they took up the statue of the goddess and carried her to Rome; and the statue seemed light and easy to move, as though the goddess went with them willingly and of her own accord.

For several years after this, the city of Veii was left standing with empty houses and temples, uncared for either by the gods or men. Some of the old neighbors of the Veientians, however, tried to make a stand against the Romans, even though Veii itself had fallen. So Camillus was sent against one of these cities, to lay siege to it, as he had done to Veii.

JUNO.

This place was also a strong city, and the people seemed likely to defend themselves as long and as bravely as the Veientians had done. But, one day, the war suddenly ceased, and peace was made, as a result of the just dealing of Camillus with the people of the besieged city.

Several of the noblest families of the city had placed their boys in the charge of a schoolmaster, who was expected not only to teach them, but to care for them during their playtime also. Before the war began, this man had been in the habit of taking his boys beyond the city walls for play and exercise, and even when the city had been besieged he continued this custom.

One day, when they had passed through the gates as usual for their romp in the open field, and while the boys were all absorbed in their rough play, their teacher led them little by little up to the Roman lines, and to the tent of Camillus. Then, as he came before the Roman general, he said:

"Camillus, these are the children of the men who are highest in rank in the city. With them I deliver to you the city itself, for their rulers will be willing to sacrifice everything to regain their children; and I know that you will reward me for my deed."

When Camillus heard these words, he cried out:

"Wicked as thou art, thou hast not come with thy offering to a commander or a people like thyself. We do not carry arms against defenseless children, but against armed men."

Then he ordered the man's arms to be tied behind his back; and he put rods in the boys' hands, and told them to flog their treacherous master back to the city; where he was punished as he well deserved to be.

When the people of the city received their children again from Camillus, their feeling toward the Romans changed. Before this time, they had preferred the fate of the Veientians to making peace with the Romans, but now the virtue of Camillus filled them with admiration. They sent messengers to the Roman Senate, therefore, and surrendered themselves without further struggle, saying:

"Fathers, we are overcome by your good faith, and we give the victory to you of our own free will. We believe that we shall live more happily under your rule than we do now under our own laws; so send men to receive our arms, and our city."

By two such victories as these, and many smaller ones, Camillus became one of the greatest of the Romans. The citizens were grateful to him for his services to the city, and they were certain that no one could lead the Roman armies so well as he.

But Camillus was a proud man, and wished to rule the city as he did his army. Among other things, he was determined that the tenth part of the spoil of Veii should be given to Apollo, as he had promised before the battle, and this the people did not wish to do. But he forced it from them; and then they asked him, in return, what right he had to the great bronze doors which he had brought from the conquered city, and placed before his own house.

So Camillus and the people fell to quarreling, and, after a time, Camillus was forced to leave Rome. In rage and in sorrow, he went to find his home in another place; but it was harder for him to bear than if he had lost his life in battle, for to be obliged to live in exile was worse than death to a Roman.

XIII

The Coming of the Gauls.

IN all the wars which the Romans had fought up to this time, they had been fighting with people who were near neighbors to them, and who were like themselves in speech, and manners, and ways of fighting. But six years after the capture of Veii, the Romans were called upon to meet a new race in battle, whose like they had never seen before, and at whose hands they met a terrible defeat.

North of the peninsula of Italy, you will remember, and shutting it off from the rest of Europe, lies the great snowy chain of the Alps. These mountains are higher and more difficult to cross than any of the mountains of our own country; but there are now many well-made wagon roads through the Alps, and even some railroads. In the early days of Rome, however, there were no such roads, and the great snow-covered ridges made a barrier which people rarely thought of crossing. The Romans knew nothing of the people who lived on the other side of the Alps, and would, perhaps, never have thought for many centuries longer, of climbing through their rough passes to find out what lay beyond them.

But the peoples who lived north of these mountains were very different from the Italians, and were not held in one place by the love of their lands and homes.

They had villages and towns of their own; but these were poor and ill-made, compared to the Italian cities, and the people were always ready to leave them to follow their chiefs into other countries to gain new possessions. The Alps, too, are easier to climb from the north than from the south, for the slope on the northern side is much more gradual. So, some of these peoples found their way over into Italy while the Romans were still thinking only of their own city, and their little neighborhood wars. These tribes from the north had many different names among themselves, but the Italians usually called them by the name of "Gauls."

GALLIC SOLDIER.

The Gauls were very different in appearance from any people that the Italians had ever seen. The Romans and the other Italians were small people compared with the Gauls, and had black hair and eyes, and dark skins browned by the hot suns of the long Italian summers. The Gauls were from the north, where the milder sunlight and the cooler summers had left their hair and skins fair and their eyes blue. This was a continual wonder to the darker Italians; and, when we add that the Gauls were larger and heavier in body than the Italians, you will not be surprised to find that the Romans spoke with awe of the blue-eyed giants, for many years after the Gauls had all disappeared from the neighborhood of Rome.

The dress of the Gauls was also strange to the Romans. They wore garments checked and striped in many colors, which remind us of the bright tartans in which the Highlanders of Scotland clothed themselves for centuries, and of which they make some use even to this day. Indeed, the Highlanders are, perhaps, the most closely related to these ancient Gauls of any people now in the world, and only a few hundred years ago, they were using war-horns and swords in their battles very much like the ones that the Romans tell us the Gauls brought with them into Italy.

The Gauls differed as much from the Romans in their manner of fighting as they did in their appearance. The Romans, during their long experience in warfare, had learned to draw up their soldiers in a regular form, with the cavalry and the infantry in fixed positions, and they always went into battle in an orderly manner. The Gauls never dreamed of anything like order in their fighting. Each man, with his broad, unpointed sword, and long shield, took his place in the great mass of his fellow soldiers; and, when the signal for battle came, they all rushed furiously at the enemy. Those who were behind pushed on those in front, if they showed signs of giving way, and their savage yells and the din of their horns terrified the enemy as much as the blows from their heavy swords.

Some tribes of the Gauls had been settled in the northern part of Italy for a long time before the Romans heard anything about them. You must understand by this time that the Romans lived in a much smaller world than ours is to-day. In a very short time, we now hear of almost everything that happens on the earth,—at least of everything within the reach of the railroads and the telegraph. But, in those days, the Romans had no way of getting word even from the different parts of Italy.

So it was only when a band of the Gauls,—leaving their families behind them, with their relatives who had settled in the valley of the Po,—pushed down farther to the south, and crossed the Apennines, that they came to the knowledge of the Romans.

These Gauls were terrible destroyers; and, as they went, they left a broad path behind them, in which there were only ruined towns, and fields bare of any sign of life. City after city fell into their hands, and when they came to the Tuscan town of Clusium, where Lars Porsena had ruled a century before, messengers were sent to Rome to beg for help against this new enemy.

At first, Rome only replied to this request by sending three ambassadors to treat with the Gauls. When these ambassadors and the men of Clusium met the chiefs of the Gauls, they asked them why they had come in this manner into the country of another people.

"We want land for those of us who have none," replied the Gauls, "and the men of Clusium have more than they can use. Give us what we ask, and we will not make war upon you."

Then the Romans cried out, thinking of their own lands, which might be asked for next:

"What right have you to ask for land from the men of Clusium, and threaten war if they refuse it?"

"We carry our right in our swords," the Gauls replied. "All things belong to the brave. Do you stand by, O Romans, and see us decide this matter with our arms, and then carry home the story of how much the Gauls excel all other peoples in bravery."

The people of Clusium could not endure this haughty speech. They refused the demand of the Gauls, and a battle almost immediately began. The Roman ambassadors, too, were angry, and this caused them to forget the law of nations, which does not allow ambassadors to fight. They entered the battle, side by side with the soldiers of Clusium, and one of the three killed a chieftain of the Gauls in the sight of both the armies.

Then the Gauls were much enraged. With a sudden impulse, they gave up their attack on Clusium, and sent messengers to Rome to demand that the offenders should be given up to them for punishment; and when this was refused, they marched straight upon that city.

The Romans heard of their coming, and prepared to meet them, but not so carefully as they would have done if the Gauls had been the people of some neighboring city. They did not seem to think it worth while to appoint a Dictator, as they had so often done when other dangers threatened them. They did not realize that they would have to meet an enemy more difficult to face than any they had ever fought before. Perhaps they even despised the Gauls for their savage ways, and their clumsy weapons, of which they must have heard; and thought that it would not be so difficult to defeat men who fought with their heads unprotected by helmets. But, if the Romans despised the Gauls before they met them, they learned from them one great lesson,—that it is never safe to scorn an enemy, until you have learned what he can do.

When the Gauls had come as near as the eleventh milestone from the city, the Romans went out to meet them with a large army. The battle took place on the banks of a little stream which flows into the river Tiber. There the Romans drew up their army in a long line, as they were in the habit of doing when they met their Italian enemies. But this was not the way in which to meet the Gauls.

As you know, the Gauls had but one way in which to fight, and that was to rush blindly at their enemy, careless whether they met death or not. It was in this way that they charged at the Roman line. With their horns blowing and their shouts rising in a fearful roar, they dashed in a great mass at the Roman army, and went through the line of brave soldiers with a rush that could not be resisted. The Romans were divided into two parts, as if a wedge had been driven through their lines; and, terrified at the savage attack and their sudden defeat, they fled blindly, as they had so often caused their own enemies to flee.

The greater part of the Roman army was cut off from Rome by the force of the Gauls, and the men were obliged to throw themselves into the Tiber, and swim to the other shore, where they took refuge behind the walls of the deserted city of Veii. The smaller part retreated in a panic to Rome; and, rushing through the city, without stopping even to close the gates, the defeated soldiers made their way into the citadel on the Capitol, which was the strongest hill of Rome.

The Gauls did not pursue them. They were amazed at their sudden success, and they hesitated to go on, for fear lest there might be some trap prepared for them. They turned back, to gather up the arms of the Roman dead; and then they spent their time in dividing the spoil and feasting. As a result of this, it was not until the third day after the battle,—in the hot days of July, three hundred and ninety years before Christ was born,—that the army of the Gauls appeared before the gates of Rome.

XIV

The Gauls in Rome.

MEANWHILE, all was terror and dismay in Rome. Only a handful of men had returned out of the army that had marched out on the day of the battle. But the Romans had not only to sorrow for the dead; they had also to fear for the living; for the men who remained in Rome were too few to defend the wide extent of the city walls against the attack of these fierce barbarians.

So, without making any attempt to defend the wall, the Romans determined to make their stand on the Capitol. This was a rocky hill, in the midst of the city, and it was well fitted for defense. Its sides were so steep, except on the one side up which the road wound, that it seemed as though no enemy could climb them. Upon it was a well, to give them water; and there, too, were the temples of the gods, to protect and encourage the Romans in their defense.

While the Gauls gathered their spoil and feasted, the Romans hastened to bring provisions to this place and prepare it to withstand a siege. Not all of the people, however, could find refuge here. No one was wanted on the Capitol who could not do his share in its defense; the women and the children, and the people untrained to arms, would only have taken the food from the mouths of those who labored to save the most sacred part of the city.

So, while the Capitol was being made ready, great numbers of the people went out of the city, and sought refuge in the hills on the other side of the Tiber, and in the neighboring cities. With them went the Vestal Virgins, carrying the sacred fire from the altar, and the vessels used in the worship of the gods. And the Romans loved to tell, in later days, how a poor plebeian, who was flying with his goods and family, met the Vestals as they were toiling along the road on foot; and, seeing their weariness, he bade his wife and children get down from his cart, that he might take up the holy maidens and carry them to a place of safety.

There were some of the Romans, however, who could not fight, and yet who would not leave the city. These were the old patricians, who were too feeble to bear arms and be useful in the citadel, but who could not bear the thought of leaving their homes and wandering in exile, while the city they loved was laid in ashes by the barbarous Gauls. They determined, therefore, to make a sacrifice of themselves to the gods for the good of their country. They were men who in their earlier years had been consuls, or had filled other high offices in the city. Now they put on their robes of state, and seated themselves in their ivory chairs in the Forum, and awaited calmly the coming of the enemy.

When, at last, the Gauls entered the city, they passed wonderingly from street to street through the empty town, seeking the enemy who awaited them only in the citadel above. When they came to the Forum, they were struck with amazement at the sight of so many noble-appearing old men, sitting there in perfect order and silence. On their part, the old men neither rose at their coming, nor so much as turned their eyes towards them, but sat gazing at one another quietly, and showing no sign of fear.

For a while, the Gauls stood wondering at the strange sight, and did not approach or touch the Romans, for they seemed more like an assembly of the gods than men. But, at last, a Gaul who was bolder than the rest drew near to one of the old men, and, putting forth his hand, he gently stroked his long, white beard. Perhaps he intended no harm; the old Roman, however, took this for an insult, and, raising the long staff which he carried in his hand, he struck the Gaul a heavy blow with this over the head.

Then the anger of the Gauls flamed up, and the old men were put to death; but this they had expected when they prepared themselves as a sacrifice to the gods. The houses of the city were then broken into by the Gauls, and robbed of the goods that had been left in them. At last, fire was set to the city, and soon its streets and buildings were a mere mass of smouldering ashes.

But even then, the Gauls could not take the Capitol. The great rock was steep and well defended, and they soon found that they could not force their way to the top. They were obliged to settle down in the ruined city and besiege the Romans. This, however, was not the kind of fighting they were used to; they always found it unpleasant to sit still before an enemy and try to starve him into surrender. Indeed, in this case, there was some danger that they might starve themselves; for they soon used up all the provisions that had been left in the town, and then, from day to day, they had to send out parts of their army to gather in food from the surrounding country.

One of these parties wandered, on one such trip, as far as the town where Camillus was then living, in exile from his native city. Though he had been badly treated by the Romans, Camillus was grieved at the misfortunes that had come upon his city. When the Gauls came into his neighborhood, instead of planning how to escape them, he tried rather to punish them for what they had done to Rome; and, taking the young men of the city, Camillus fell upon the camp of the Gauls by night, and destroyed them entirely.

When the news of this act reached those Romans who had taken refuge in Veii, they began to recover from their terror, and to plan for the rescue of Rome. But first they must have a leader; and where, they asked, could they find a better one than Camillus, who had captured Veii for them, and had just shown them how to overcome the Gauls?

Before Camillus could become their general, however, he had to be recalled from exile, and appointed to be their leader by the Senate. What was left of the Senate was besieged on the Capitol at Rome; so the men at Veii sent a youth to that place with messages to the Senate, asking that they would recall Camillus and appoint him to command them.

This messenger boldly traveled the greater part of the way to Rome by day, but he waited until night to draw near to the city. Then he passed the river by swimming, with pieces of cork under his garments to hold him up, and approached the Capitol. Here, at a place which the Gauls had left unguarded, he managed to scramble up its rocky side, and reach the top in safety. Then he delivered his message to the Senate, and they granted his request gladly, and named Camillus, Dictator. After that the youth returned as he had come, bearing his message back to Camillus and to the men at Veii.

The next day some of the Gauls at Rome found the marks of hands and feet where the messenger had climbed the side of the Capitol. Then they said to one another:

"Where it is easy for one man to get up, it will not be hard for many, one after another."

So the next night they made the attempt. Sending an unarmed man ahead to try the way, they followed in his steps, passing their weapons from one to another, and drawing each other up over the steep places. In this way, they reached the top, and reached it unnoticed by the Romans. The sentinels were fast asleep, and even the dogs were quiet and gave no alarm.

But the sacred geese that were kept near the temple of Juno were more watchful. As the enemy approached their inclosure, they cackled loudly and flapped their wings, and this awoke an officer named Marcus Manlius, who was sleeping near by. At once, Manlius snatched up his arms, and, shouting to awake his comrades, he rushed to the spot where the first Gauls were just climbing over the wall of the citadel. One of them he slew with his sword, and another, at the same time, he struck full in the face with his shield, and hurled him headlong from the rock; and this man, as he fell, threw down others who were below him. And now Manlius's companions had joined him, and spears and stones fell thick and fast upon the climbing enemy; and soon the last of the attacking party was dashed to ruin at the foot of the rock, and the citadel was saved.

THE CAPITOL AT ROME.

After this, the siege continued for many months, and it bore heavily on the Gauls and the Romans alike. Both sides reached the limit of their endurance at last. It was the time of the year which was most unhealthy in Rome—the late summer and autumn—and many of the Gauls fell sick and died, for they were used to a colder and more healthy climate.

The Romans were in a still worse condition, for their food was giving out. Even when Marcus Manlius had saved the Capitol, the Romans could do no kinder thing for him in return than to give him each half a pound of corn and half a pint of wine, taking this from the nourishment of their own bodies that he might be rewarded. Now there was not even this to give, and they had looked long and vainly for Camillus and the promised help from Veii. They were wearied with constant watching; and their bodies, weakened by hunger, could scarcely bear the weight of their arms.

So, at last, when the Gauls offered to break up the siege, and leave Rome in return for a thousand pounds of gold, the Romans were ready to consent. Then they brought out the gold to the Gauls for settlement; but, as the Gauls weighed it in the scales, the Romans charged them with balancing the scales unfairly. The only answer of the Gallic chief to this charge was to unbuckle his heavy sword from his waist, and throw it —belt, scabbard, and all—into the scale with the weights; and when the Romans indignantly asked the meaning of this, he calmly replied:

"What should it mean but woe to the conquered?"

The Romans could do nothing but add the gold to make up the extra weight. They were conquered, indeed.

XV

Rebuilding the City.

THE stories go on to tell us that, before the Gauls got well away from Rome, Camillus arrived at last and defeated them, and took back the gold which had been given them as a ransom. It is likely however, that this is only what the Romans wished could have happened, and not what really took place.

But, whether the Roman gold went with the Gauls or not, a very much heavier trouble had fallen upon the city, for the town was in ashes, and the people were scattered far and wide. It had taken hundreds of years to build Rome, and but a few months to destroy it. How the men and women must have mourned as they came back from their hiding-places and saw only heaps of stone and ashes where they had left their streets and homes! Only the Capitol lifted its head in the midst of the blackened ruins, bearing its buildings and temples unharmed.

Those who were in the greatest despair, as they gazed at the ruined town, were the common people. They had lost all of the little which they had possessed; and, as they looked at the ruins around the Capitol, they shrank from the task that they saw before them. Rome must be begun anew; and what toil it meant for them only to clear the ground and make ready for the work of building! And, after that was done, the greatest work would yet remain,—the gathering of the material and the building of the houses.

Many of the people had returned from Veii, where they had been living in the well-built houses of that city, and they thought of them with regret.

"Why should we remain here, O Romans," cried the leaders of the people, "and toil at this great work? A home awaits us in Veii, ready built and with most fertile fields around it. That city was conquered by us from our enemies; let us make use of it now in our great need."

Then the people, looking at the ruins about them, cried:

"Yes, let us go! Let us begin anew in Veii!"

But they did not go. When Camillus heard of the plans of the people, he went to them, with the whole Senate following after him, and he spoke to them with these words:

"What is this that you think of doing, O Romans? Why have we struggled to recover our city from the Gauls, if we ourselves desert it as soon as it is recovered? Shall we now leave the Capitol, which the Romans and the gods still held, while the Gauls lay camped in the city? Shall even the citadel be deserted, now that the Gauls are fled and the Romans victorious? We possess a city founded by the gods; not a spot is there in it that is not full of them. Will you forsake them all by leaving Rome? Shall the Virgins forsake thee, O Vesta, and the priests of Rome become Veientians? Has our native soil so slight a hold on us, or this earth which we call mother? Does our love of country lie merely in the surface, and in the timber of our houses? For my part, I will confess to you, that, while I have been absent from my city, whenever it came into my thoughts, all these occurred to me,—the hills, the plains, the Tiber, the face of the country, so familiar to my eyes, and this sky, under which I have been born and educated. May all these now, by your love of them, induce you to remain, rather than that they should cause you grief and regret after having left them. Not without good reason did gods and men choose this place for founding a city,—these most healthful hills, and this large river bearing the fruits of the inland country to us, and ours to the sea,—this place in the center of Italy. The very size of our city before it was destroyed is a proof of its good situation. Where is the wisdom of your giving this up, now that you have proved it, to make trial of another city into which good fortune may not follow you? Here is the Capitol, which it was foretold should become the chief seat of empire. Here is the fire of Vesta. Here are the shields of Mars, let down from heaven. Here are all the gods, who will be favorable to you if you stay."

In spite of the speech of Camillus, however, the people still hesitated, and the Senators even could not quite decide what it would be best for them to do. But, as the Senate was still discussing the matter, an officer marched through the Forum with his soldiers, and called out:

"Standard-bearer, fix your standard. Let us halt here."

His words reached the ears of the Senators as they sat, in anxious quiet, in the Senate-house near by. It seemed to them like a message from the gods, commanding them to remain at Rome. They came out of the Senate-house, therefore, exclaiming that "they accepted the omen"; and the common people, when they were told of the occurrence, allowed themselves to be persuaded to remain.

Then the Senate ordered that Veii should be destroyed, so that the people should never again be tempted to leave Rome; and the materials were brought from Veii to Rome, and used in building the city anew. The Senate also gave the people liberty to take wood and stone for building free of charge, and to build their houses wherever they could find a place. So, within a year, the city was rebuilt, after a fashion; but the houses at first were poor and mean, and the work was done so hurriedly that no attention was paid even to the course of the streets. This made the streets of the new Rome very narrow and crooked, as they wound about among the buildings; and even the sewers, which before the Gauls came had followed the line of the streets, were now built over with private houses.

STANDARD-BEARER.

The Romans were not allowed to rebuild their city in peace, however. All the peoples around them began to take advantage of their weakness to prevent them from growing strong and powerful once more. As we read the old stories, we wonder whether the Romans would have ever succeeded in restoring their city if it had not been for Camillus. He led them against their enemies many times, and always with success; and often he gained the victory for them more by the enemy's fear of him than by the size of his armies or the strength of their arms.

At last, Camillus had grown to be an old man of eighty years, and when a call to battle came he feared that he was no longer fit to lead the Romans to victory. The citizens, however, would not allow him to retire from the command; for his mind was still clear and strong, and they thought that that was worth more than youth and strength of body.

So Camillus went forth from Rome, with another man—Lucius Furius—for a companion in command; and he led his men cautiously to the seat of the war. The enemy had more men than Camillus had, and were awaiting him in a city which had belonged to the Romans before the coming of the Gauls. When they saw the Romans approaching, they came out and offered to give battle immediately; for they thought that, by doing this, they would give Camillus less chance to plan his battle skilfully. But Camillus was too wise in the art of war to be caught in any such way, and he prepared to keep his men from battle until he saw a good chance for victory.

This made the enemy all the more eager, and they

came close to the Roman camp and began digging trenches and preparing for battle as though daring them to fight. This was hard for the Roman soldiers to bear, even though they were so few in number compared with the enemy. In their anger, they began to think that Camillus was holding them back more because of the weakness and fears of age, than from carefulness for their safety and for the victory. The other general, the young Furius, was of this opinion also, and did not hesitate to say what he thought among the soldiers.

"Wars are the business of young men," he said, "and it ought to be so, for, in the best condition of the body, the mind is strongest also. Why should Camillus now hold his men quiet in the trenches when formerly he used to carry camps and cities at the first onset? What increase does he expect to his own strength; what falling off does he hope for in the enemy? Camillus has had a goodly share of years, as well as of glory. Shall we now allow the strength of the state to suffer because his body sinks into old age?"

When the soldiers, excited by these words, demanded battle, Furius went to Camillus, and said:

"Camillus, we cannot withstand the violence of our soldiers, and the enemy insults us in a way not to be endured. Do you, who are but one man, yield to all, and allow us to do as we wish, that the victory may be ours the sooner."

Then the old Camillus replied:

"Whatever wars have been fought, up to this day, under my single care, have not proved either my judgment or my good fortune to be wanting. But now I have a companion in my office of general, who is my equal in command and my superior in the vigor of youth. I have been accustomed to rule the violence of my army, not to be ruled by it. But with my companion's power I cannot interfere. You may do Lucius Furius, that which you think best for the interest of Rome. I beg only one thing, and that is, that, in consideration of my years, I may not be placed in the front rank. Whatever duties of war an old man may discharge, in these I shall not be found wanting. And I pray the immortal gods that no misfortune may come upon the Romans to prove that my plan would have been the better one."

Then the Romans were drawn up in battle order and advanced to the attack, leaving Camillus, as he had desired, with some reserve troops in the camp. The old general first posted strong guards about the camp, and then stood anxiously watching the advance of the Romans.

As he had feared, he did not see them gain a victory. At first, the enemy seemed to give way, and the Romans followed eagerly. But when the retreating soldiers had drawn them on to where the ground was difficult, they suddenly faced about, and others of their men joined them, and they attacked the Romans at a disadvantage. It was not long before Camillus, from the high ground from which he watched the battle, saw the Roman line break and the soldiers turn and fly toward his camp.

Then Camillus commanded his men to lift him on his horse, and, calling to his troops, he led them out against the enemy. When he met the Romans rushing blindly back, he cried:

"Is this the battle that you called for so eagerly, soldiers? Why turn your faces toward the camp? Not a man of you shall my camp receive, except as victor! Having followed another leader, now follow Camillus, and conquer as you have done before, when I lead."

At this the soldiers halted, stopped at first by shame. Then when they saw their old general, whom they had followed to so many victories, go forward against the enemy in the front rank, they turned and joined him, with shouts and renewed courage. And once more Camillus led them on to victory.

You would think that, after this battle, Camillus would be angry with Lucius Furius. But this was not the case. He seemed to wish to forget that it was the bad judgment of Furius that had brought on the battle, and to remember only that he had fought with the greatest bravery through it all.

"This day," said Camillus, "will be a lesson to him not to prefer his own plans to better ones."

So, when Camillus was appointed general for a new war soon after this, he chose this same Lucius Furius as his companion in command; and they went out together, once more, in friendliness and good fellowship.

Do you remember when, in his earlier days, Camillus could not remain at Rome because he could not live without quarreling with his fellow-citizens? Now you see him forgiving a real injury, and showing only kindness to the man who had scorned him in his old age. Camillus had learned something better, during his long life, than how to lead his soldiers to victory; for he knew how, at the last, to return good for evil, and to make a friend of one who might have been his enemy.

Camillus lived for some years longer, and when he died the people felt as though they had lost a second Romulus; for he had almost founded their city a second time, by persuading them to remain in it after the retreat of the Gauls, and by protecting them from their enemies while they rebuilt their dwellings. The wisdom of his desire to remain at Rome was seen even before his death, for the city had already sprung up in a vigorous new growth; and we now believe, as Camillus did then, that nowhere else could Rome have grown to be the great city which it finally became.

XVI

The New Rome.

IT is not an unusual thing for a city to recover after such a misfortune as the sack of Rome, and become greater than before. In our own country such a thing has happened. Your father, perhaps, remembers when the city of Chicago was burned in 1871, and all the country was called upon to send food and clothing to the thousands of people who had lost their homes and all they possessed. But now Chicago is the second city in size in the United States, and all because of ceaseless labor and endeavor since that time. Rome did not recover from her misfortune so rapidly as Chicago did from hers, for she did not receive such generous help from the country around her. You have seen that the neighbors of Rome would have preferred to injure, rather than to aid, the people of the destroyed city. But, thanks to the wisdom and skill of Camillus, and the determination of her people, Rome at length recovered from her misfortune, and became a powerful city once more.

In one way their troubles were a good thing for the Romans. The patricians found it so important, for their own good, that the common people should stay at Rome and help in the work of rebuilding the city, that they became willing to give up many of the rights which, before this, they had kept to themselves. It was not many years after the new Rome had been built that a man from the plebeians was elected consul, along with a man of noble birth. This was a great victory for the common people, and it was soon followed up by others. Before a century had passed, from the burning of the city, the plebeians were allowed to hold any office to which a patrician could be elected, and the old distinctions between the classes were entirely removed.

In spite of the fact that Camillus had called their hills "most healthful," Rome was troubled for many years after the rebuilding of the city with much illness among the people. You will remember that the Gauls sickened quickly in Rome; and now, even the citizens themselves, who were used to the climate, sickened and died in great numbers. This indeed was the cause of the death of Camillus himself, after all his long years of fighting on Roman battlefields; and sometimes there was so much sickness among the people that the armies could not be sent out against their enemies as usual.

This trouble was caused partly by a lack of good water in the city. The well-water about Rome, and also the water of the Tiber, was impure; and the cisterns did not furnish enough for the use of the people. The Romans must have felt this need very keenly, for, while they were fighting battles on every side, they set themselves to work to bring in a good supply of water from outside the city, as is now done in all our large towns. Eight miles out from Rome there were hills where pure water could be found in plenty, and they brought this into the city in a passage which they built for it under ground.

Such a passage for water they called an "aqueduct," and we still use the same word ourselves, having borrowed it from the Romans. The reason that they

RUINS OF A ROMAN AQUEDUCT.

did not, at first, build their aqueducts above the surface of the ground was that they feared lest, at some time, their enemies might succeed in turning the stream aside, and thus leave the city without water. But as Rome conquered her enemies about her, and the city grew larger and needed a greater supply of water, many new aqueducts were built, and these were built above ground. Even to this day, you can see, near Rome, the remains of some of the great stone troughs—sometimes high up in the air on stone arches—in which water was brought from miles away to the city of Rome.

At this time, also, the Romans began a work which was as great as the building of their aqueducts. This was the making of good roads.

As soon as the Romans began to send out armies to fight with the neighboring cities, they must have seen the need of well-built roads that could be used through all the seasons of the year, and in wet and dry weather alike. Such roads became still more necessary now that the Romans had come to rule lands and cities lying many miles from Rome. So while the Romans were bringing good water into Rome, they began their first long road; and the man who led them in building their aqueduct was also foremost in making this road. His name was Appius Claudius, and he was quite as great a man as any of the Roman generals that we are told so much about. Because the road was built under his direction, the Romans named it the "Appian Way," after him, and even to-day what remains of this road is still called by this name.

From the beginning, the Romans built their roads with the greatest care. First, after they had removed the earth to the proper depth, they placed a layer of large flat stones on the ground. Then a layer, nine inches thick, of smaller stones, was laid upon these, and cemented together with lime. Next came a layer, about six inches thick, of still smaller stones, and this too was bound together with cement. And, at last, on top of all, blocks of very hard stone were laid, and fitted closely together, so as to make a perfectly smooth surface on which to drive or walk.

Is it any wonder that roads built with such care have lasted for two thousand years?

This building of roads and bringing of water into the city was not a small thing for the Romans to do, as

A ROMAN ROAD.

perhaps it may seem now, when well-paved streets and waterworks are to be found in almost every large city. The Romans did this when such things were only beginning to be thought of by men, and they did it so well that they set an example which the whole world has been glad to follow ever since. They saw what they needed, then they thought out the best way to meet their wants, and then, last of all, they were willing to work hard and long in order to do well whatever they undertook. It is this as much as anything else which made the Romans become one of the greatest peoples that the world has ever seen. They thought well and worked hard, whether it was in fighting battles or building roads, and in the end this made them the masters of the world.

The Romans not only thought things out for themselves, however; they were always ready to learn from others as well. Whatever they saw that seemed good to them, they borrowed and made part of themselves. They learned from the Etruscans a great deal of that knowledge of building which they used in constructing their temples and aqueducts. When, for the first time, they went to war with an enemy beyond the sea, the Romans learned how to build war-vessels from a ship of the enemy which was wrecked on their shores. When the Romans found that the short, straight sword, which the people of Spain used, was better than their own, they armed their soldiers with that. And when they found that the Greeks were better poets and artists than they were, the Romans took them to be their teachers in poetry and in art.

But, besides the power of the Romans to think, to work, and to learn from others, there was something else that made their city strong. This was the love and devotion of her people. The best of the Romans were willing to die for her, and did die for her, not only by going into battle and laying down their lives there, but in other ways as well.

Old writers tell us that once a great chasm, or hole, many feet deep, suddenly opened in the Forum at Rome. This must have been caused by an earthquake, such as those which often occur even now in Italy, and sometimes in our own land. The Romans were greatly distressed by this chasm, and they tried to fill it by throwing earth into it. But, in spite of all their efforts, the opening would not be closed. Then they could only look upon the chasm as a work of the gods, and they asked the priests the meaning of it, and how it might be filled. The priests replied:

"Search out what is the most precious thing of the Roman people, for that is what must be thrown into the chasm in order to satisfy the gods and make sure that the city will last forever."

Then, as they questioned among themselves what this "most precious thing of the Roman people" might be, Marcus Curtius, a youth who had done great deeds in war, exclaimed:

"Can you doubt what this means? Is there any greater good for Romans than arms and bravery? This is what the gods demand; and I will devote myself as a sacrifice to them, so that my country may never perish."

Then he put on his richest armor and mounted his horse and rode to the edge of the chasm, while the people of Rome crowded the Forum and stood watching. When he had prayed to the gods, Curtius leaped his horse into the opening, and horse and rider disappeared from sight. After that the chasm closed, and all that was left to show where the opening had been was a little pool of water, which the Romans named the Curtian lake, in honor of this youth who had so willingly and gladly sacrificed himself to the gods for the good of the Roman people.

At another time, a Roman named Decius Mus did

something very much like this act of Curtius. Decius was consul, and was leading the army in battle when he saw that the Romans were giving way and the enemy was pressing on to victory.

"Valerius," he cried, to the chief priest who stood by him, "we have need of the aid of the gods. Come! tell me the words by which I may offer myself a sacrifice for my soldiers."

Then, with his head covered and leaning on a spear, he repeated these words after the priest:

"Janus, Jupiter, Father Mars, and all ye gods under whose power we and our enemies are: I pray you that you will grant strength to the Roman people, that they may strike the enemies of the Romans with terror, dismay and death. I devote the soldiers of the enemy together with myself to the gods of the dead, for the sake of the soldiers of Rome."

He then mounted his horse, and rushed into the midst of the enemy, where he fell pierced by many weapons. The Roman soldiers, who followed him in his attack, were victorious; and they thought that the gods had given them the victory because their consul had offered himself as a sacrifice for them.

XVII

The War with Pyrrhus.

IF you will look again at the map of Italy, you will see that the Apennine mountains run from the northwestern part in a great curve through the peninsula. Within a hundred years after the Gauls destroyed Rome, the Romans ruled all the lands around the city between these mountains and the sea. But they had not yet crossed the mountains to the north; and they had no thought of going beyond them in the south either, until something happened there which forced them to do so.

The southern coast of Italy was not occupied by Italians, but by Greeks, who had come across the sea from Greece long, long before, and built cities on the southern shores of the peninsula. They were a gay, changeable people, who had now grown to be very much less worthy in character than the old Greeks who had fought the Persians so well in former days. They preferred to hire soldiers to fight for them, instead of fighting for themselves; for they loved the bustle and chatter of their city life, and the amusement of their open-air theatres, more than anything else in the world.

The most important of these Greek cities in Italy was Tarentum, which lay on the western side of the heel of the peninsula. There the people had built their theatre in a place which overlooked the sea; and as they were gathered here one day, they saw ten Roman war vessels approaching the city harbor.

Now, there was an agreement between the Romans and the people of Tarentum that the Roman war ships should not sail beyond a certain point on the southern shore; so, when the Tarentines saw these vessels coming in close to their town, they were very angry. They did not stop to think that the Romans might be coming peacefully, and with no thought of harm. They rushed headlong from the theatre to the shore, and got aboard their ships and rowed out to attack the Roman vessels; and, as the Romans were entirely unprepared for battle, five of their ships were sunk, and the men were taken prisoners.

The other five ships managed to escape, and when they returned to Rome with the news of how they had been treated at Tarentum, the Romans were very indignant. But they did not want to go to war with the people of Tarentum; so, instead of sending an army to attack that city, they sent ambassadors to demand an explanation of the wrong that had been done them.

When these ambassadors reached Tarentum, they were led before a large body of the citizens, in order that they might state their business in the hearing of all. Their grave manner and broken speech, as they tried to make their meaning clear in the Greek tongue, amused the Tarentines immensely. They laughed at them and mocked their blunders, and, at last, one wretched fellow threw dirt on the clean white toga of one of the ambassadors.

At this, the Greeks laughed louder than ever; but the insulted Roman raised the stained folds of his toga and held them before the eyes of the people.

"Laugh on, now," he cried; "but the stain on this gown can only be washed out with blood."

Then the ambassadors departed, and the two cities began to prepare for war,—but in what different ways! The Romans gathered their men together as usual, and sent them under the command of a consul across the mountains into southern Italy. But the Tarentines did not think of getting ready to fight themselves; that was not their fashion. The only thing they did was to send over into Greece to hire some general there to bring an army to fight for them against the Romans.

There were many men in the Grecian peninsula at this time who were willing enough to fight, and who knew how to fight well; but the man to whom the Tarentines sent was especially ready to give the help that they asked.

This was Pyrrhus, the king of one of the little countries of western Greece, who was a brave and generous man, and one of the best generals of that time. He was related to Alexander the Great, who a few years before this had become the conqueror of Greece and of much of the world besides. From his very boyhood Pyrrhus had lived with the Greek armies at home, in Asia, and in Egypt; and he had determined that if he should ever have the chance he would try to become like Alexander—a conqueror of great nations. So now, when the Tarentines sent to him and begged his help against the Romans, he readily gave his consent, and began to plan victories for himself in the west as great as those which Alexander had won in the east. For he meant not only to help the Tarentines against Rome, but to bring all the Greek cities of Italy and of the island of Sicily under his rule at the same time.

When Pyrrhus had gathered his army together and sailed to Tarentum, the foolish people of that city suddenly discovered that they had given themselves a stern ruler where they had only asked help against their enemy. The king had no patience with their lightness and gayety in such a time of danger. He closed their theatre and public meeting-places, and set the people to work helping his soldiers in their task of preparing for the Romans. The Tarentines obeyed unwillingly; perhaps they were already beginning to wish that they had not been so rash in making trouble, or so ready to ask aid when the trouble had come.

Soon after Pyrrhus reached Italy, the two armies—the Greek and the Roman—met in battle near Tarentum. On both sides, the men fought so bravely that for a time it could not be told which would gain the victory. The Greeks formed their men in one solid mass, drawn close together with their shields touching and their great spears, eighteen feet long, extending far out in front of them. The Romans formed their men in many small companies, which were arranged loosely into three ranks, one behind the other; in this way, each company and each rank could act separately, while all supported one another. The Greeks were the strongest in defending themselves on a level surface, for the Romans could scarcely break through the dense hedge of their spear-points, and get near enough to reach them with their short swords. But the Romans could attack their enemies more freely than the Greeks could, and they could move more easily over rough ground.

In this battle, the Romans rushed time and again at the solid ranks of the Greeks, and seemed determined never to give up the effort to break through and throw them into disorder. But Pyrrhus had with him in his army something of which the Romans had never seen the like before. This was a herd of elephants; and when these huge beasts charged upon the Romans, with towers upon their backs filled with armed men, the Romans were filled with dismay and drew back, and their horses went mad with fright, and turned and trampled down the Roman lines. Then the Romans retreated in confusion, and the battle was lost.

A ROMAN SOLDIER.

Pyrrhus had gained the first victory, but he saw that he had met enemies who could not be despised, even though they had been defeated. When the fight was over, he stood upon the battlefield and saw the Roman dead all lying with their faces turned toward the enemy.

"If these were my soldiers," he said, "and I were their general, I could surely conquer the world."

After this battle, Pyrrhus sent his trusted friend

Cineas to Rome to propose terms of peace to the Senate, for he thought that the Romans would now be ready to give up the war.

This Cineas was as great as a statesman as Pyrrhus was as a general, and it was said of him that his tongue had taken more cities for his master than Pyrrhus had taken with his armies. During his visit to Rome, Cineas made himself most agreeable to the citizens. He had such a good memory that, after one day in Rome, he could call every great man by his name; and he was such a good judge of men that he never failed to treat each person in the way that would be most pleasing to him. So all the Romans liked him, though he was their enemy; and the Senate was almost persuaded by him to do as Pyrrhus wished, and settle upon a peace.

But there was one person in Rome whom Cineas could not win over. This was Appius Claudius, who had constructed the first aqueduct and had built the Appian Way. He was now an old man, gray-haired and blind, and it had been a long time since he had gone from his home to take his place in the Senate. But when he heard that the Senate was about to make peace with Pyrrhus, he commanded his servants to take him up and carry him in his chair through the Forum to the Senate house. There his sons and sons-in-law met him at the door, and when he was led in and rose to speak, he was received with a respectful silence.

"Until this time, O Senators," he said, "I have borne the misfortune of my blindness with some impatience. But now, when I hear this dishonorable purpose of yours, it is my great sorrow that, being blind, I am not deaf also. To make peace with Pyrrhus will be to destroy the glory of Rome. Do not persuade yourselves that making a friend of Pyrrhus is the way to send him back to his country. It is the way, rather, to show the world that you can be conquered in one battle; and soon other invaders will be upon us. The true way to rid us of our dangers is for Rome never to treat with a foreign enemy while his army remains in Italy."

The Senators were shamed by the noble courage of the aged Claudius. Instead of making peace with Pyrrhus, they sent Cineas back to his master with the message that they would not treat with him about terms of peace and friendship until his army was removed from Italian soil; and they added that so long as he stayed in Italy under arms, they would continue to fight with him, even though he should defeat them many times.

This noble answer of the Romans impressed Cineas very much. When he returned to Pyrrhus, and the king asked him what he thought of the Romans and their government, he answered:

"The Roman Senate, Sire, is an assembly of kings."

Pyrrhus himself soon had a chance to see the spirit of one of the Romans of that day. The Senate sent Caius Fabricius to the king, shortly after this, to treat for the return of the Roman prisoners who had been taken by the Greeks. Cineas told Pyrrhus that Fabricius was one who stood very high among the Romans, as an honest man and a good soldier, but that he was very poor. So Pyrrhus received him with kindness, and tried to bribe him with gold. But Fabricius refused to accept the king's gifts.

"If I am dishonest," said he, "how can I be worth a bribe? And if I am honest, how can you expect me to take one?"

Then Pyrrhus tried him in another way. The next day he commanded that one of the largest of the elephants should be placed behind the curtains while he and Fabricius sat talking together. At a signal from the king, the curtains were drawn aside, and the elephant, raising his trunk just over the head of Fabricius, trumpeted loudly. But the Roman only turned quietly and said to Pyrrhus:

"Neither your money yesterday, O King, nor this beast to-day, can move me."

You can understand that after this Pyrrhus admired Fabricius greatly. To show his favor to him, he allowed him to take the Roman prisoners with him when he returned to Rome; for a great festival in honor of the god Saturn was about to be celebrated, and all Romans wished to take part in it. And Fabricius, in return, gave his promise to the king that if the Senate did not agree to make peace, the men should all come back to him when the holiday was past.

This festival to Saturn was held each year in the latter part of December, and was a sort of Thanksgiving festival. It was a time when the Romans gave presents, as we do now at Christmas time, and the poor people received gifts of corn and oil and wine, and watched the servants of the wealthy carry baskets of nuts and figs and apples to their masters' friends. It was a happy, joyous time, when the boys all had new tunics and new shoes, and the slaves were allowed to be equal to their masters for once in the long year.

The festival must have passed all too quickly for the prisoners of Pyrrhus; for the Roman Senate again refused to agree to a peace, and they were sent back to the Greeks as soon as the festival was over. The Senators were so anxious to keep the promise of Fabricius unbroken, that they commanded that any prisoner who should remain behind should be put to death; but this order was not needed, for they all returned faithfully to their captivity.

It was not long after this till the Romans and the Greeks met again in battle. Once more the Romans were defeated; but they fought as stubbornly as they had in the first battle, and again it was only the elephants that won the victory for Pyrrhus. After the battle, one of the friends of the king came to him and wished him joy over his victory. But Pyrrhus replied, seeing the large number of his own men who had fallen:

"One more such victory as this, and I am lost."

The king was thinking how far he was from his own country, from which he had brought all his best soldiers, and how difficult it would be to fill up the vacant places in his army with men who were as good as those he had lost; for the Greeks of Italy did not make good soldiers. It was different with the Romans. Among them every man was a soldier, and as soon as one army was destroyed, another one as large and well-trained could be raised to take its place.

After this second battle, Pyrrhus did not care to fight again with the Romans. He left Italy and went over to the island of Sicily, and tried to make himself master of the cities there. He remained in the island for three years. When he returned to Italy, he found that the Romans had made good use of his absence. They had gained all the southern part of the peninsula except the city of Tarentum; and they were now in better condition to give battle to him than ever.

The Romans had seen that the close ranks of the Greeks fought best upon a level surface; so, when a third battle with Pyrrhus took place, they placed themselves on rough, uneven ground. The Romans had also lost much of their fear of the elephants by this time; and, when the great beasts charged at them in this battle, they hurled darts and spears at them, and so wounded and vexed the animals that at last they turned and rushed back upon the Greeks themselves. In this way the solid mass of Pyrrhus's soldiers was broken up, and after that it was not long until his whole army was terribly defeated.

After this third battle, Pyrrhus was obliged to leave Italy and go back to his own country, a disappointed man. He had failed to conquer an empire in the west, as he had planned; and it was the Romans who had caused his plans to fail.

Not long after he had gone, the city of Tarentum itself fell into the hands of the Romans; and after the fall of that city, Roman rule reached throughout the whole of Italy, from the toe of the boot up to the valley of the River Po in the north.

XVIII

Rome and the Carthaginians.

NOW that the Romans had become masters of almost the whole of the peninsula of Italy, you might expect that their wars would cease, and that they would be left to govern peaceably what their arms had won. But this was not to be the case. As you will see, the Romans had soon to prepare for a struggle which was to prove the longest and hardest that they ever went through. This was due to the fact that right across the Mediterranean Sea from Italy, there was another people who had also been able to make themselves rulers over other lands and nations; and, after the Romans had conquered the Greeks of southern Italy, there was no longer any state to stand between these two proud and powerful peoples.

This other people dwelt in the city of Carthage, and were called Carthaginians. Their city was founded more than a hundred years before Romulus began the first settlement on the Palatine hill; and now Carthage was a larger and richer, as it was an older, city than Rome; and its people ruled a great part of the coast of Africa, of Spain, and of Sicily, and most of the islands of the western Mediterranean.

The people of Carthage were Phœnicians, and their mother country was along the eastern shores of the Mediterranean. They were of the same race as the

Jews, who dwelt near by the mother land in Palestine; and in speech and religion they were more different from the people of Rome than any other people that the Romans had ever come in contact with, except the Etruscans. They were a nation of sailors and traders, and their ships were the best then known to men. They were the first to discover that they could steer their vessels, when out of sight of land, by using the North Star to guide them; so, while other nations still kept safely in sight of the shores of the Mediterranean in their voyaging, the Phœnicians pushed boldly out into the broad Atlantic, and sailed as far as the island of Great Britain on the north, and on the south a good distance down the coast of Africa. They were the discoverers and traders of that long-ago time; and they made settlements, too—just as the English, and French, and Spanish did in later days,—wherever they could find a good harbor, with a fertile country around it, or with mines of gold or silver or tin to work. And they did more, even, than this. In order to keep their records and accounts, they invented the alphabet which we use to-day; and they taught these letters to the Greeks and the Romans, though the languages which these people wrote with them were different from that which the Phœnicians used.

So, when the Phœnicians left their old home to found a new city in the west, they brought with them much useful knowledge. Their children, too, and their children's children, made good use of what their fathers had brought. By the time this story begins, Carthage had become a great city, which was said to cover twenty-three miles of country; and the sails of its ships dotted the waters of the western Mediterranean. The Carthaginians were good builders, also, as well as good sailors and traders. They had protected their city on the land side by three great walls, one inside of the other, and these walls were far stronger and better built than the walls which surrounded Rome. The space between the walls was taken up with stables for the elephants and war horses, and here were kept three hundred of the one and four thousand of the other. And to shelter the many ships of the Carthaginians, two great harbors had been dug out, in addition to the natural bay on which the city was built,—one for the trading vessels, and one for the ships of war.

The Carthaginians were not only a powerful people; they were also very jealous of their power, and wished to prevent any other people from sharing in it. They looked upon the sea, on which their many vessels came and went, as belonging to themselves alone; and when they found the ships of other nations sailing in their waters, they did not hesitate to capture the vessels and to drown the men that they found on them. They are even said to have boasted once that, without their permission, the Romans could not even wash their hands in the waters of the sea.

The struggle between the Romans and the Carthaginians began in Sicily. The Carthaginians had long had possession of the western part of the island, while the eastern part was ruled by a number of Greek cities. It was to take the part of these Greek cities against the Carthaginians that Pyrrhus had gone to Sicily; so the Carthaginians were friendly to Rome until the Romans had driven Pyrrhus back to his eastern home.

As soon as he was disposed of, however, the friendship between Rome and Carthage began to cool. Pyrrhus had foreseen that this would be so; and as he had left the island of Sicily he had looked back at its shores and exclaimed:

"What a field we are leaving for the Romans and the Carthaginians to contend in!"

Just across the strait which separates Italy from Sicily, was a Greek city which soon after this got into very serious trouble with one of its neighbors. The people in the city were divided as to what they should do for help; so one party sent to Rome for aid, while the other invited the Carthaginians in. Now, the Romans could not permit the Carthaginians to become settled so near to Italy as that was, and, rather against their will, the Romans were forced to send the aid which had been asked. The result was the first war between Rome and Carthage.

Although the Carthaginians were masters of the sea, they were not prepared to fight the Romans on land. They had no army of citizens to depend on, such as Rome had. They hired their soldiers, as you will remember the Tarentines did, and gathered them together from many different countries. So it took them a long time to get a strong army ready to fight in Sicily; and in the meantime the Romans won many victories and took many important towns from them.

But the Romans soon discovered that they could make few lasting gains in fighting against the Carthaginians, without a navy to help them. They might conquer all Sicily with their armies, but when the war vessels of the Carthaginians came sailing around the island, the cities on the coast which had given themselves to the Romans would have to go back to the Carthaginian side once more. Besides this, the Romans—who had almost no war vessels and very little experience in managing them even if they had had them—seemed to be unable to get at Carthage itself to do it any serious harm. But the ships of Carthage could dash in from the sea upon the coast of Italy, and destroy a city or ruin a whole stretch of country before the Italians could make a move to defend themselves.

When the Romans saw this, they did one of the most daring things that we read of in their history. They determined to build a fleet, and go out and meet the Carthaginians on the sea, where they had so long been masters. They took for their model a Carthaginian ship that had been wrecked on their shores, and within sixty days, the old writers say, a growing wood was changed into a fleet of one hundred and twenty ships.

While the vessels were building, they had also to find rowers for their new fleet, and to train them for their work. To do this, rows of seats, arranged one above the other, like the benches of rowers in a ship, were built upon the ground; and on these the men took their places daily, and were taught to move their great oars all together, in obedience to the voice of the rowing master. Then, when the ships were done, the men were given a short time to practice on the water the movements which they had learned on the land; and after that the fleet sailed away to Sicily to seek out and fight their enemies.

But for all their bold and determined spirit, the

Romans knew very well that they could not, for some time, hope to be a match for the skilful Carthaginian sailors. Their hastily-made ships were clumsy and hard to manage, and the green wood of which they were built was already beginning to warp apart and let in the water. Their rowers and sailing-masters did not

NAVAL BATTLE.

know how to make the best even of the poor ships they had; and for knowledge of the sea itself, and of its storms and currents, and of the harbors of its coasts, the Romans had to depend upon people of other cities, whom they hired to help them. The only way that the Romans could hope to win a sea-fight was by getting their vessels right up alongside the ships of the enemy, and then fighting it out with their spears and swords, just as they would a battle on the land.

To enable their vessels to do this, some clever Roman thought out a plan which all the ships adopted. A strong mast was planted in the prow of every Roman vessel, and about this was fastened a long plank or platform, in such a way that the outer end of the plank could be pulled up and let down, like the drawbridge of a castle, in front or on either side of the vessel. At the end of the plank, and pointing downward, a long spike was fixed, so that when the plank was let fall this spike would sink into the deck of the enemy's ship and hold it fast. When the platform was raised against the mast, this sharp piece of iron sticking out in front looked so much like the strong bill of a great bird that the Romans called the whole thing a "crow."

When the Carthaginians saw the Roman ships sailing up to meet them, they were puzzled at first by the strange structures in their bows; but they knew that the Romans were ignorant of everything that had to do with managing ships, so they supposed that they would have an easy victory. They rowed straight out to meet the Romans, therefore, and sought to ram the Roman vessels with the prows of their own ships. But no sooner did a Carthaginian vessel come within reach of a Roman one, than down fell the "crow" of the latter, and the two ships were held firmly together. Then Roman soldiers poured across the bridge thus made, and soon they had captured the vessel. In this way the Romans captured or destroyed fifty of the Carthaginian ships, and those that were left were glad enough to turn and flee from the terrible Roman "crows."

This was the first Roman victory on the sea, but after it they won many others. Now that they had a fleet, moreover, the Romans could take an army across the sea to Africa, and there fight the Carthaginians in their own land. This they did; and the Roman general, Regulus, was very successful there for a time, and, at last, brought the Carthaginians so low that they were forced to ask for peace.

Then Regulus showed how little he knew the brave people with whom he was fighting. He seemed to think that Carthage was as completely conquered as the little Italian towns which Rome had been taking, one by one, for so many years. The terms of peace which he offered were so hard that the Carthaginians concluded that they could not be left in a worse condition even if Carthage itself was captured; so they resolved to continue the war. Fortunately for them, the Carthaginians now found a good general, who knew how to use their cavalry and their elephants. Soon Regulus himself was defeated and taken prisoner; and for five years he was kept a captive at Carthage while the war continued on land and sea.

It had been thirteen years since the Romans had first crossed over into Sicily, when ambassadors were again sent to treat about peace. According to the stories which have come down to us, Regulus was now taken from his prison and sent to Rome, along with the Carthaginian ambassadors, to assist them in bringing about the peace; and he was made to promise that if peace was not made he would return at once to Carthage.

The Carthaginians sent Regulus with the ambassadors because they thought that, for his own sake, he would do all that he could to help bring the war to a close. But when Regulus reached Rome, he was noble enough to forget himself in his love for his country. He advised the Senate not to make peace, and not to exchange their Carthaginian prisoners for the Romans who were in the hands of Carthage; and in the speech which he made in the Senate he is reported to have said:

"Let not the Senate buy with gold what ought to be won back only by force of arms; and let those Romans who surrendered when they ought to have died in battle, die at last in the land that saw their disgrace."

When Regulus said this, he knew that if he went back to Carthage after such a speech, the Carthaginians would put him to death. For a while the Senate hesitated, out of pity for him; but at last the peace which the Carthaginians asked was refused. Then Regulus went quietly back to Carthage, as he had promised; and if we may believe the story, the Carthaginians cruelly put him to death, as he had expected that they would do.

For ten years longer, the war dragged on, until at last neither Carthage nor Rome had money or men to spend in further efforts. Rome had been most unfortunate at sea. Fleet after fleet which she sent to Sicily and Africa was wrecked and destroyed by the terrible storms which rage there at certain seasons of the year, and which the Romans did not know how to guard against.

After this had happened several times, the Romans

determined to make one more effort. Their ships were all gone, and there was no money in the treasury to build new ones; but the wealthy citizens of Rome joined together and built a fleet of two hundred vessels at their own expense; and they only asked, in return, that if the city could ever repay them, it would do so.

With this fleet the Romans again set out, and this time they were as successful as they had been the first time they took to the sea. They had now learned from their mistakes and misfortunes, while the Carthaginians had become careless; so, when the Romans came up with the Carthaginian fleet off the western coast of Sicily, they sunk fifty of the enemy's vessels and captured seventy more.

Then Carthage and Rome made peace, for they saw that neither city could wholly conquer the other, at that time. Carthage had got the worst of it in this first war; so she was obliged to give up all claim to Sicily, to release the Roman prisoners without a ransom, and besides this, to pay to Rome a large sum of money for the expenses of the war. Rome took possession of the part of Sicily which the Carthaginians had held, and set up a government over it; and before many years had gone by, the whole island had passed under her control. In this way arose Rome's first possession outside of Italy.

XIX

The War with Hannibal.

AFTER the Carthaginians had made peace with Rome, and had withdrawn their troops from Sicily, they had to endure three terrible years of warfare with their own subjects and soldiers, in the country round about Carthage. But through all this time of defeat and disaster, there was one man among them who remained undismayed.

This was Hamilcar, the greatest of their generals and the only man among the Carthaginians whom the Romans at that time feared. Hamilcar had fought Rome successfully, as long as his city could give him money and men to fight with; and when he saw that Carthage could do no more, it was he who had made the peace. He had no thought of a lasting peace with Rome, however; he hated that city as much as he loved Carthage, and he was already planning a way to injure her, while he made up to his own country for the loss of Sicily. Both of these objects he thought he could gain by conquering the Spanish peninsula, where the Carthaginians had already made settlements; and when he brought the matter before the Senate at Carthage, they gave him permission to take an army there and see what he could do.

As Hamilcar was preparing to leave for Spain with his army, he went before the altar of one of the

Carthaginian gods, and offered sacrifice for the success of his plans. During the sacrifice, his little son Hannibal, who was then about nine years old, stood beside him; and when it was over, Hamilcar turned to the boy and said:

"Hannibal, would you like to go with me to Spain?"

When the lad eagerly answered that he should like very much to do so, Hamilcar took him by the hand and led him to the altar, and said:

"Then lay your hand upon the sacrifice, and swear that you will never be friends with Rome, so long as you shall live."

The boy did as he was bidden; and in due time he was taken away to Spain, with the thought deep in his breast that he was now the enemy of Rome forever. From that time, he grew up in the camp of his father, and his daily lessons were in the arts of war and of generalship. He was his father's companion while Hamilcar conquered the rich peninsula of Spain for Carthage; and before Hamilcar had died, Hannibal had learned all that his father could teach him of warfare and of government.

After Hamilcar was gone, Hannibal proved himself a worthy son of so great a father; and when he was only twenty-seven years of age, he was chosen to fill his father's place as commander of the Carthaginian army. This army was made up, in large part, of men from the conquered nations in Spain; but under the leadership of Hannibal, it did not matter much who the soldiers were who made up the army. His men became simply the soldiers of Hannibal, and were so filled with love and admiration for their general, that they were ready to follow him anywhere and do anything that he commanded.

When Hannibal had got his army in good condition, he attacked a town in Spain that was friendly to Rome, and conquered it. The Roman Senate was already beginning to fear this son of Hamilcar as it had feared Hamilcar himself, and when news came of the attack on this friendly town, it sent ambassadors to Carthage to demand that Hannibal should be given up to the Romans. But the Carthaginians would not consent to this. Then the leader of the Roman ambassadors gathered up the folds of his toga and held them before him, saying:

"I carry here peace and war; which shall I give to you?"

"You may give us whichever you choose," replied the Carthaginians.

"Then I give you war," cried the Roman, as he shook out the folds of his toga.

In this way, the second war between Rome and Carthage was declared. But it was not really a war between the two states which now began. It was rather a war between all the power of Rome, on the one side, and Hannibal, with his devoted army and his vow of hatred to the Romans, on the other. When Hannibal heard in Spain that war had been declared, he was prepared for it, and needed only to think how he should attack his enemies.

He was determined that this war should be fought on Roman, and not on Carthaginian, ground. That meant that the war was to be fought in Italy. Hannibal had the choice of two ways of reaching Italy from

Spain. He might cross the sea in Carthaginian ships, or he might go by land, through Spain and Gaul. If he chose the latter way, he would have to make a long march through an unfriendly country, and cross the Alps, which are the highest mountains in Europe. If he chose to go by sea, he ran the risk of wreck by storms, and defeat and capture by the Roman fleet,

HANNIBAL.

which was now stronger than that of the Carthaginians. Either way, it was a choice of evils.

Hannibal chose to go by land; but we may be sure of one thing, and that is, that he did not know quite how difficult a path it was that he had taken. He was the greatest man of his time, but he had no good way of learning the simple facts about the world he lived in which you are taught in every day's geography lesson. The thought of the mountains to be climbed, and the rivers to be crossed, in the long journey, did not make him hesitate, for he did not fully know them. He knew that the Gauls had passed through the high Alps, —then why could not he do it also? He could have had no clear idea even of the distance his soldiers would have to march before they reached Italy; for his guides at any time could tell him the way and the distances for only a few days' march ahead, and when that was passed he would have to find other persons who knew the country beyond, and would undertake to guide his army on.

In was in the month of April that Hannibal started on his long march. Besides the many thousand men, both infantry and cavalry, who made up his army, he took with him thirty-seven of the Carthaginian elephants to use in battle, and many horses and mules to carry the baggage of the army.

As soon as he got out of the territory that had been conquered by Carthage, his troubles began. He had to fight his way against unfriendly natives through northern Spain; and it was midsummer before he had crossed the mountains which separate the peninsula from Gaul. Then, in a short time, he came to the swift-flowing river Rhone. Here the Gauls gathered on the opposite bank, and tried to prevent him from crossing. Hannibal soon overcame these enemies, however, and led his army safely over in canoes and boats, which his men collected along the river; but the elephants could only be taken over after he had prepared great rafts on which to ferry them across.

After they had crossed the Rhone, the way was easy until they came to the foot of the Alps; but there the greatest difficulties of the march began. The way now lay along steep, narrow paths, up which the horses and elephants could scarcely climb; and often a single slip or misstep would have been enough to send them rolling and tumbling a thousand feet down the mountain side, to be dashed to pieces on the rocks below. The people who inhabited the mountains, too, were unfriendly to the Carthaginians. They stationed themselves on either side of the zigzag path up which the army toiled, and hurled stones and weapons upon them from the heights above. These threw the long line of baggage animals into great disorder, and the wounded and frightened horses galloped back and forth, and either fell themselves or crowded others off over the cliffs and down the mountain side, carrying with them as they fell baggage which the army could ill afford to lose. Again and again Hannibal was obliged to take some of his best men and clamber up the cliffs and over the rocks to attack and drive off these enemies; and once in such an attempt he and his men were separated from the rest of the army, and were forced to remain on their guard all night long under the shelter of a great white rock which stood by the side of the path.

At last, on the ninth day after they had begun their ascent, the army reached the summit of the pass. After that they were no longer troubled by attacks from the mountain tribes. Here Hannibal remained for two days, in order to rest his men and beasts; and while the army was here, many of the horses which had taken fright and run away, and many of the beasts of burden, which had got rid of their loads, came straggling into camp, having followed the tracks of the army.

After they had rested sufficiently, they began the descent into Italy. But now new difficulties presented themselves. The way was now down-hill, but the slope was more abrupt than it was on the other side of the mountains. It was now late in the autumn, moreover; and as the snow falls early in these high regions, the paths were already covered with a thin coating of new-fallen snow, which caused the men and beasts to slip and made the descent more dangerous than the ascent had been. At one place, too, they found that a landslide had completely blocked up the path, and it took four anxious days of hard labor to cut out a new one for the horses and elephants in the side of the steep and rocky cliff.

But, through all their trials and dangers, Hannibal cheered and encouraged the army. When they reached a height from which the rich plain of the valley of the River Po could be seen in the distance, he called his men about him, and pointing to it, he said:

"There is Italy! There are friends waiting to welcome you and aid you against the tyrant Rome! You have now climbed not only the walls of Italy, but of Rome itself; and after one, or at most two, battles, all these fertile fields will be yours."

Then the soldiers pushed on with new courage; and on the fifteenth day after they had entered the Alps, they came out on the other side of them, in Italy. But the army was terribly weakened by the hardships of the way and the fights with the natives. More than half of the men and horses, and many of the elephants, had been lost; and the soldiers who remained were so broken and worn by their sufferings that they looked not like men, but like the shadows of men.

Still, the courage of Hannibal did not fail him. He camped his men at the foot of the Alps among friendly tribes of the Gauls, and allowed them to rest and refresh themselves for several days, while the poor lean horses were turned out to pasture; and soon all were ready once more to follow wherever he chose to lead them.

The Romans had not expected that Hannibal would attempt to cross the Alps and carry the war into Italy; or, if any of them did expect it, they had no idea that he would succeed so well and so soon. So, when news came that Hannibal was already in Italy, the Romans were surprised and dismayed; but still they hurriedly gathered together their forces, and sent them on to meet the enemy.

Any one but Hannibal they might have stopped, but Hannibal they could not check. He defeated them in battle after battle, and swept on through their country, with his little army, in a torrent that could not be resisted. The Romans fought desperately, aroused by fear for the city itself; but the armies that faced Hannibal were destroyed in quick succession. In one battle the Romans lost nearly 70,000 men, including eighty senators; and the Carthaginians gathered from the rich men who had fallen on that field enough gold rings to fill a bushel measure. After that, the name of Hannibal became a word of terror to old and young alike;

and nearly two hundred years after this time, the memory of that terror still lingered. A Roman poet then wrote of him, and called him "the dread Hannibal," and said that his march through Italy was like the sweep of the eastern gales that had wrecked so many Roman fleets in the waters of Sicily, or like the rush of flames through a blazing forest of pines.

The Romans had learned how to defeat the Gauls and the Greeks in battle, but they were long in learning how to defeat Hannibal. He was greater than they, and, as long as he remained in Italy, the city of Rome trembled. But the Senate remained strong in the midst of the public terror, and while the people mourned for their dead, the Senators only sought men for another army to take the place of the one that had last been destroyed. Their generals, too, though they could not defeat Hannibal in battle, learned to be cautious; and they would no longer lead their armies out to fight against him, but hung about watching his camp, in order to cut off any of the Carthaginians who might become separated from the main body while searching for food for themselves or for their horses. In this way, they sought to wear out Hannibal by cutting off his supplies, and so make it necessary at last for him to leave Italy of his own accord.

In the end, Rome succeeded, as she always did. "The Romans," said an old writer who described this war, "are never so dangerous as when they seem just about to be conquered." Hannibal found, as Pyrrhus had done before him, that he was fighting a people who could replace a defeated army with another which was just as ready as the first to fight to the death.

Most of the peoples of Italy, too, remained faithful to Rome in this time of trial; and Hannibal was disappointed in getting the help from them, against their conqueror, upon which he had counted. So, at last, he was forced to look to Africa and to Spain for new men and for supplies for his army; and when his brother came over the Alps, bringing him help from Spain, he was defeated and slain by the Romans before Hannibal knew that he was in Italy. Besides this, the Senate found men and ships enough to carry the war over into Spain and Africa; and, by and by, the Carthaginians were forced to order Hannibal to give up his plans in Italy in order to return to defend Carthage itself against the attacks of Rome.

SCIPIO AFRICANUS.

So, after fifteen years of victories, which brought the war no nearer a close, Hannibal was obliged at last to leave Italy and return to Africa. It was the first time he had been back since he had left there, as a boy, thirty-six years before. When he arrived, he found Carthage much weakened by the war. The general in command of the Roman army there was Publius Cornelius Scipio, or "Scipio Africanus," as he soon came to be called, from his deeds in Africa. He was an able general, and had just brought the war in Spain to an end; where, as he reported to the Senate, he "had fought with four generals and four victorious armies, and had not left a single Carthaginian soldier in the peninsula." Now he was to do something greater still, something that no Roman had ever yet done,—that is, to defeat Hannibal in an open battle.

This battle took place near a little town called Zama, which was about two hundred miles inland from Carthage. Scipio had more troops than Hannibal, but Hannibal had about eighty elephants, and he hoped to win the battle with these. The Romans, however, were now thoroughly used to fighting against elephants; they opened great lanes in their ranks, and let the elephants pass harmlessly through, while the soldiers hurled spears and other weapons at them to drive them along or turn them back. Then the Roman foot-soldiers charged the Carthaginians, shouting their war-cry and clashing their swords against their shields. After a hard fight the Carthaginians were overcome. Hannibal alone, with a few of his horsemen, succeeded in escaping, and he at once advised the Carthaginian Senate to make peace.

The terms of the peace were much harder than they had been at the close of the first war. Carthage had to give up all of her possessions outside of Africa, and surrender all of her elephants, and all of her warships but ten. She had also to pay an indemnity of about twelve million dollars to Rome, and to agree never to make war on any one without the consent of the

Roman Senate. In this way, Carthage ceased to be the head of a great empire, and became merely the ruler of a little strip of territory along the coast of Africa.

After the treaty was signed, Hannibal remained at Carthage, and tried faithfully to help his country in peace as he had helped her in war. But the Romans feared him still, and distrusted him, and before many years had passed, he was forced to fly from the city to avoid being put to death by their orders. After that, he wandered about from kingdom to kingdom, on the eastern shores of the Mediterranean. But wherever he went, Roman messengers followed, and would not let him rest in peace; and, at last, after thirteen years of wandering, he was forced to take his own life to avoid falling into the hands of his unforgiving enemies.

XX

Rome Conquers the World.

THE victory which Rome had won over Hannibal meant something more to the Romans than saving their country from the Carthaginians. It meant the spread of Roman rule from Italy and Sicily over into Africa, Spain and Greece, and even into Asia. The Carthaginians were the only people of that day who were strong enough to resist the Romans for any length of time. When they were defeated, at last, there was no other nation in the world that could oppose the power of Rome successfully. Besides this, the Romans were the only people that knew how to rule well, and could put down pirates and robbers, and make the world safe for men to live in. Whenever trouble would arise in any country, the Romans would interfere; and then it would not be long before the old government would cease, and the Romans would be ruling that country as part of their own land.

Before sixty years had passed from the close of the second war with Carthage, Rome had, in this way, become the ruler of almost all the lands that border upon the Mediterranean Sea; and she had gained this great power without any one planning it beforehand, or intending to bring it about.

You have seen that the Romans received Sicily after the first war with Carthage. During the second war, while Hannibal was in Italy, they conquered Spain; and they kept it for themselves after this war was over. Then they felt the need of conquering northern Italy and southern Gaul, so that their armies could march from Rome to Spain without being attacked by

enemies on the way; and this land also was added to the Roman rule. In this way, Rome came to rule over almost all of the western part of the Mediterranean world.

It was not long before the Romans reached out into the eastern part of the Mediterranean also. Just north of Greece was a country called Macedonia, whose king had sent soldiers to Hannibal, at the battle of Zama, to aid him against the Romans. To punish him for this, the Romans made war upon him, and defeated him; and, when his son Perseus took up arms after his father's death, they defeated him also. Then the Romans began to rule over Macedonia, and over Greece as well, for the Greeks had long been ruled by the Macedonians, and were now no longer able to rule themselves. And the Romans even went over into Asia Minor and made war on a great king there, who was interfering with affairs in Europe, and who besides was sheltering Hannibal after the Romans had caused him to be driven from Carthage. In this war, the Romans were easily victorious; and, after this, all of Asia that lay along the Mediterranean came under Roman influence also.

By this time, the Roman name had become a great one throughout all the world about the Mediterranean Sea. Whenever the ruler of a country was threatened by an enemy, and was too weak to meet him alone, his first thought was to call upon the Romans for help. In this way the ruler of Egypt begged the help of Rome, when a neighboring king made war upon his country. The Senate sent an ambassador to this king, and when they met the Roman drew a circle with his staff on the ground about the king, and said:

"Before you step out of the circle which I have drawn, answer this question, O King. Which will you do, give up your war upon Egypt and have Rome for your friend; or continue it and have Rome for your enemy?"

It did not take the king long to decide that it was best to give up the war. After that the Romans had much influence in Egypt, because they had saved the country from its enemies; and in the course of time, it too was joined to the Roman lands.

In the meantime, Carthage had been slowly recovering from her last war with Rome. Once more, her streets were filled with citizens and her harbors with ships; and the city was growing strong and wealthy again. But now a stern old Roman named Cato went to Africa and visited Carthage, and, seeing the city growing prosperous once more, he feared that it might again become able to fight with Rome on equal terms. When he returned to Italy he bore away with him a bunch of fine figs, plucked in the gardens of Carthage. Upon reaching Rome, he spoke long and earnestly in the Senate of the danger which the Carthaginians might yet be able to bring upon the city, and then he showed to the Senators the fresh figs which he had brought back with him.

"The country where these grew is but three days' sail from Rome," he said. "Carthage should be destroyed."

And after this he never ended a speech in the Senate, no matter what he had been talking about, without adding, "And, moreover, I think that Carthage should be destroyed."

At last Cato persuaded the Romans to make war upon Carthage a third time. In spite of the brave defense of the city by the Carthaginians, when even the women and children joined in the fight, the Romans were victorious once more. This time the city was utterly destroyed, and the ground upon which the buildings had stood was ploughed over and sowed with salt, so that it might never more be used by men, or even covered by growing things again. Then Rome began to rule the land about Carthage, and so gained control of most of the northern coast of Africa.

In this way, the city of Rome came to hold a power in the world greater than any nation has ever held before or since that day. And in whatever country the Romans went, they made their aqueducts and built bridges and raised public buildings, as they had been doing for so long in Italy itself. Above all, they built good roads to all the lands that came under their rule, so that they might send armies swiftly from one country to another whenever there was need to do so. Along these roads they placed milestones, so that travelers might know at any time just how many miles they were from Rome; and where the towns were far apart, stations were built by the way where they might rest and hire fresh horses to carry them on their journey to the next stopping-place. In this manner, the Romans made traveling by land much easier than it had ever been before, and thus distant lands were more closely connected with one another, just as they have been in our own day by the building of railroads and the putting up of telegraph and telephone wires.

But Rome could not go out over the world and build in and rule over all the Mediterranean countries, without this making a great difference in the Romans themselves. Their great men were no longer like Cincinnatus, who left the plough to fight for his country and then went back again when the danger was past. The Roman generals were now very rich men, and they spent all their time in war or in the public business of their country. And, instead of refusing the gifts of kings as Fabricius had refused the gold of Pyrrhus, it was said that the Roman generals asked for money wherever they went about the world.

The common soldiers, too, were not so good as they had been in the old days. Then each man fought in the army without pay, and supported himself and his family in time of peace by means of his little farm. But now many men began to make a business of fighting, and to serve in the army for a living. As these men did not fight solely for the love of their country, but rather for the money that they got by it, they began to grumble when they were commanded to do things which they did not like to do, and sometimes they refused outright to do them.

With such generals and such soldiers, it is not surprising that the Romans were now sometimes shamefully beaten in battle.

When they were carrying on the war in Macedonia against King Perseus, the first armies that were sent against him were defeated for just this reason. Then the Romans saw that there must be some change made, and they chose a general of the old-fashioned sort to take the command. His name was Æmilius Paullus, and he was a poor man still, although he could easily have been rich if he had been willing to do as other men were doing. He had been one of the generals in Spain, and also in the north of Italy, and in both places he had shown that he knew how to manage his armies and to gain victories. So the people agreed that he was the man to send against King Perseus, and, rather against his wishes, they elected him consul, and voted to give him command of the army.

Æmilius did not thank the people after they had chosen him consul, as was usually done. Instead of that he said:

"I suppose, O Romans, that you have chosen me to lead in this war because you think that I can command better than anybody else. I shall expect, therefore, that you will obey my orders, and not give me orders yourselves; for if you propose to command your own commander, you will only make my defeat worse than the former ones."

When Æmilius came to the army in Greece, he saw that the first thing to do was to teach the soldiers to obey orders. He kept them in camp and drilled them for many days; and when they murmured and wanted to be led out to battle, he said to them:

"Soldiers! you should not meddle with what does not concern you. It is your business only to see that you and your arms are ready when the order is given, and that, when your commander gives the word, you use your swords as Romans should."

In this way, Æmilius trained his army; and when the battle was fought, the Romans won a great victory. King Perseus and his children and all his treasures were captured, and his country was brought under the Roman rule. But Æmilius would not so much as go to see the heaps of gold and silver which had been taken from the king's palaces. Instead of making himself and his friends rich from it, he commanded that it should all be sent to Rome and put into the public treasury; and the amount of it was so great that never after that did Rome have need to raise a war tax from her own people.

The common soldiers, however, were angry at this action of Æmilius, for they wanted to divide this spoil among themselves; besides this, they disliked him because he ruled them so strictly. So, when the army had returned to Rome, and it was proposed that Æmilius should be allowed a triumph, the soldiers opposed the motion before the people. But an old general who had commanded in many wars arose, and said:

"It is now clearer than ever to my mind how great a commander our Æmilius is; for I see that he was able to do such great deeds with an army full of baseness and grumbling."

At this, the soldiers were so ashamed that they let the people vote the triumph for Æmilius.

When the day for the celebration came, seats were set up in the Forum and in all parts of the city where the show could best be seen. On these the Roman people took their places, dressed in white garments and ready for the great holiday. The temples were all open and filled with flowers and garlands, and the main streets were cleared, and kept open by officers who drove back all who crowded into them. Then came the great procession, which lasted for three days.

On the first day, two hundred and fifty chariots passed, filled with pictures and statues and other images which had been taken from the Greeks.

On the second day, the rich armor which had been captured was shown; and it made a fine sight, with the light glancing from the polished helmets and shields, and with the swords and spears rattling about among the armor. After the wagons bearing this, marched

TRIUMPHAL PROCESSION.

three thousand men, each bearing a basin full of silver coin; and after them came others, bearing the silver bowls, goblets and cups which had been taken.

But the third day was the finest sight of all. First, early in the morning came the trumpeters, sounding such notes as the Romans used to encourage their soldiers in battle. Then came young men wearing robes with ornamented borders and leading one hundred and twenty fat oxen, all with their horns gilded, and with ribbons and garlands of flowers tied about their heads. These were for the sacrifices to the gods, which were to be offered at the temples on the Capitol; and with them went boys bearing basins of gold and silver to be used by the priests in the offerings.

After the cattle for the sacrifices came seventy-seven men, each carrying a basin filled with gold coin; and with them marched those who carried the golden goblets and dishes which King Perseus had used at his table. Then came the chariot of the king, with his armor in it, and his crown lying on top of that. Then came the king's little children—two boys and a girl—with their attendants and teachers; and, as they passed along, the attendants wept and stretched out their hands, and begged the Romans to show mercy to the little princes. Many hearts were touched at the sight of this misfortune of tender children.

Then, after a little space, came King Perseus himself, clothed all in black, and walking quite alone, so that all the people might get a good look at him. After the king and his attendants had gone past, Æmilius himself appeared, riding in a splendid chariot, and dressed in a robe of purple mixed with gold, and holding in his right hand a laurel branch. And following the chariot marched all the army, with laurel branches in their right hands, and singing songs of triumph,—just as though they had been the most obedient soldiers in the world. So the triumph ended.

Many years before, you will remember, the Roman people had crowded the Forum to see Marcus Curtius leap into the chasm and sacrifice himself for the good of his country. What a different sight they had now come to watch—their great army coming home in triumph, burdened with the wealth of a conquered kingdom, and the king and his little children walking into a cruel captivity before the chariot of their general! The power of Rome had indeed grown greatly in the meantime; but if we could have seen both sights, perhaps we should have decided that, after all, the first one was the better for the Roman people.

XXI

The Gracchi and Their Mother.

AFTER having watched the splendid triumph of Æmilius, let us see one of the more common sights of the city,—a Roman wedding. You will find it very unlike the weddings you may have seen among our own people, but, however strange the Roman customs are to you, you must remember that they were very sacred to the Romans.

Imagine that you are a Roman, and that it is your sister who is to be married. First, she is dressed in a garment made all of one piece of cloth, without any seams, and fastened about the waist with a woolen belt or girdle. Her hair is curled in six little curls, and it must not be parted with a comb, but with the point of a spear; and about her head she wears a yellow veil or net. In the evening, a procession is formed by the friends of both families, and the bride is taken from her father's house to that of her husband; and along the way minstrels play on their harps, and bridal songs are sung, and a little boy marches on before, carrying a blazing torch made from the wood of the white-thorn tree.

When the procession comes to the door of the bridegroom, the bride must wrap the doorposts with sacred fillets of white wool, and smear them with oil or fat. After that she must be carefully lifted over the doorsill by her husband. Some of the older people will tell you that this is done so that the bride may not stumble as she enters her husband's house for the first time, for that would be a very bad sign; but others will say that this is done in memory of the time when the followers of Romulus took wives from among the Sabine women by force.

After the procession has entered the house, the bride turns and says to her husband:

"Where thou art, Caius, there will I, Caia, be also."

After these words, the husband presents her with fire and water, to show that she is now a member of his family, and can sit at his hearth and join in the worship of his household gods. After this comes the feast, with its wedding cake and plenty of nuts scattered about; and then the wedding is over.

This is the way that Cornelia, the daughter of Scipio Africanus, was married to Tiberius Gracchus. He was a fine soldier and a just and honorable man; and she was then a beautiful girl, with bright clear eyes, that showed a noble soul within.

For many years they lived happily together, and had many children. Then, according to the story, he found in their sleeping-room one day a pair of large snakes. Now, the Romans looked upon snakes as something sacred; so Tiberius Gracchus went to the priests and asked what he should do with them. The priests answered that he must kill one of the snakes and let the other go; and they added, that if he killed the female snake, Cornelia would die, and that if he killed the male, he himself would shortly perish.

Tiberius loved his wife very much; so, when he

heard this, he went home and killed the male snake, and let the female escape. And shortly after that he himself died.

After that, Cornelia lived only for her children; and when the king of Egypt sent to her and wished her to become his queen, she would not consent. Only three of her children—two boys and a girl—lived to grow up to manhood and womanhood; and on these Cornelia centered all of her love and care. She lived with them, and played with them, and taught them their letters; and, as she was a noble, high-minded woman, her children grew up to be brave, honorable and truth-telling in all that they did.

One day, as Cornelia was sitting at home, with the children playing in the courtyard within, a lady came to visit her. As she talked with Cornelia, this lady showed her the splendid rings and precious stones which she wore, and at last asked to see Cornelia's jewels.

Then Cornelia called her little children, and when they stood before her and her visitor, she said:

"These are my jewels."

As her boys grew up to be men, Cornelia would sometimes reproach them that she was still known as the relative of the Scipios, and not as the mother of the Gracchi; and in this way she made them long to do great deeds, so as to bring her honor.

The oldest of the two boys was named Tiberius, after his father. When the time came for him to enter the army, he went at his work with so much earnestness that in a short time he excelled all the other young men in deeds of arms.

When the Romans made war on Carthage for the

third time, Tiberius Gracchus was the first man to get up on the wall of the city; and when he was in Spain, helping to carry on a war with the mountain tribes that lived in that peninsula, he saved the whole army from being destroyed as a result of the faults and mistakes of its commander.

But it is not for what he did as a soldier that we remember Tiberius Gracchus most frequently. It is rather for what he did after he returned to Rome and became a tribune of the people.

During the terrible war with Hannibal, the small farmers had their farms ruined, and fled to the city. After the war was over, the land gradually passed into the hands of the Senators and rich men of Rome, and a few great farms took the place of many small ones. The worst of it was that these large farms were not tilled by free laborers, but by slaves, just as the land in the southern states was before our Civil War—except that the Roman slaves were white, and were treated ever so much more cruelly than our negro slaves ever were. So the poor freeman not only lost his land, but he lost the chance to work for hire also. The only thing he could do after that was either to enlist in the army and earn his living as a soldier, or else remain idly at Rome and cry out for bread to keep him alive and games to amuse him; and the rich candidates for offices were so eager to get the aid of the poorer citizens that they gladly bought their votes by feeding and amusing them. But, in this way, both the rich and the poor became selfish and greedy, and thought only of what would help themselves, instead of what would be best for the whole people.

·

Tiberius Gracchus saw these evils, and when he became tribune, he tried to cure them. Much of the land which the rich men held really belonged to the state, though it had been out of the hands of the state for so many years that the people who held it had begun to forget that they did not really own it. What Gracchus proposed to do was to take back this land, and divide it among the poor citizens, and so build up once more a strong class of small landholders, such as had made Rome fit to be a conquering nation.

The men who already had this land did not like this plan at all; so, when Gracchus brought forward his law for the people to vote on it, they got another tribune, named Octavius, to veto it, and that stopped the voting. Then, when Gracchus found that he could not get Octavius to withdraw his veto, he got the people to put him out of his office and elect a new tribune in his place. This was against the law, but Gracchus did not see any other way of getting his measure passed.

After this, the law which Gracchus had proposed was passed, and he and two other men were appointed to carry out the distribution of the lands. Before the work was done, however, Gracchus's year of office was up; and he was afraid that as soon as he should be out of office, the rich citizens would not only find some way to stop the carrying out of the law, but they would also punish him for putting Octavius out of office. It was against the laws, at this time, for any one to be tribune two years in succession; but Tiberius decided to disobey the laws once more, and get himself elected tribune a second time.

When the Senators and rich citizens heard this, they

were very angry, and determined to prevent it. When the day of the election came a riot broke out. Gracchus was accused of trying to make himself king. Then the Senators and rich men armed themselves with clubs and bits of benches and stools, and set upon the poorer citizens; and Tiberius Gracchus and three hundred of his followers were slain.

Gracchus had been wrong in putting Octavius out of office, and in trying to get himself elected tribune a second time against the laws. But how much worse was the action of the Senators and rich citizens! In the old days, when the patricians and the plebeians struggled together, they did so peaceably and with respect for the laws. Now, in these new struggles between the party of the poor and the party of the rich, force was for the first time used and men were killed in a political struggle at Rome; and for this the Senators and rich men were chiefly to blame.

Caius Gracchus was not at Rome when his brother was killed; he was, moreover, still a very young man, and had just begun his training in the army. For ten years longer he went on serving with the armies of Rome. Then, although the Senate tried unlawfully to keep him from returning to the city, he came back, and he too was elected tribune.

Caius was much more hot-tempered than his brother had been. In spite of all that his mother Cornelia could do to prevent it, he resolved to carry out the plans of his brother Tiberius, and even to go further. He wanted to overturn the government by the Senate and the nobles, and put in its place a government by the people, with himself at their head. He got the support of the people for this by passing a law that they should always have grain sold to them at a low price. Then he got the support of many of the rich citizens, by passing laws which took rights and privileges from the Senators and gave them to the rich men who were not Senators.

In this way, Caius Gracchus got much more power than his brother had had; and a law having now been passed which permitted one to be re-elected as tribune, Caius was made tribune a second time. After this, he was able to pass many laws to help the poorer citizens. But when he wished to go further, and to help the Italians who were not citizens of Rome, then the Romans selfishly deserted him. They were afraid that they would have to share their cheap grain and their free games with the Italians, so this law was not passed; and, at the next election, Caius Gracchus was not made tribune again.

After that Gracchus tried to live quietly, as a private citizen, at Rome. But now that he was no longer tribune, the nobles soon found means to pick a quarrel with him; and when a riot again broke out, Caius and many of his friends were put to death by the Senators, as Tiberius Gracchus had been before them.

You would think that, after the death of her second son, poor Cornelia would be heart-broken and would never want to see Rome again, because of the ingratitude with which its citizens had treated her sons. But the Romans believed that you ought not to show sorrow at anything that might happen to you, no matter how dreadful it was. So Cornelia put on a brave face, and hid the suffering which was in her heart; and when she spoke of the deeds and deaths of her sons, she spoke of them without a sigh or a tear, just as if she were talking about some of the ancient heroes who had died ages before. So all men admired her for her courage and virtue; and in time the Roman people repented of their conduct towards her sons, and began to look upon them as the truest friends they had ever had. And when Cornelia died, a statue was set up to her, and underneath it were carved these words, as her best title to fame:

"Cornelia, the mother of the Gracchi."

XXII

The Wars of Caius Marius.

CAIUS MARIUS was a poor country lad who entered the army as a common soldier and, without the help of money or of a powerful family, rose to the highest position. It is said that when he was a boy, he one day caught in his cloak an eagle's nest, with seven young ones in it, as it was falling from a high tree. From this the wise men foretold that he should be seven times consul; and Marius never rested until this saying came true.

He gained his first knowledge of war in Spain under Scipio Æmilianus. This Scipio was the son of Æmilius Paulus, the conqueror of Macedonia, and had been adopted into the family of the Scipios by the son of the great Scipio Africanus; as he was also an able and honorable man, he was thus a very good master under whom to learn the art of war. Caius Marius profited well by the lessons which he learned in the camp of Scipio. And when Scipio was asked one day where the Romans would ever find so good a general as himself when he was gone, he turned and touched the shoulder of young Marius, who stood by, and said:

"Here, perhaps."

This encouraged Marius, and he struggled on for many years, gradually rising in the army and in the state from one position to another. At last the opportunity came when he could get himself elected consul, and have the command of an army himself.

The opportunity came in this way. A king named Jugurtha arose in a little kingdom near Carthage, who gained his power in a most unjust manner, and then used it in a way that was even worse. At last the Roman Senate was forced to declare war upon him. He did not prove to be easily conquered, and the Roman generals who were sent against him did not seem to be able to bring the trouble to an end. At last Marius, who was with one of the generals as second in command, became very impatient over this delay in crushing Jugurtha, and resolved to go to Rome and try to get the command for himself.

Now Marius was very well liked by the common soldiers because he had been one of themselves, and also because he ate the same coarse food and slept upon the same beds that they did, and would often help them with his own hands in digging ditches and throwing up earthworks. But the general of the army laughed at him because of his low birth; and when Marius applied to him for permission to go to Rome to become a candidate for consul, he said:

"It will be time enough for you to become candidate for consul when my young son does."

This angered Marius; and when he came to Rome he told the people how slowly the war was going on and how much better he could carry it on. As he was one of themselves, the common people believed him and elected him consul, and by a special vote they gave him the command of the army against Jugurtha.

When Marius returned to Africa, he found that it

was more difficult to bring the war to an end than he had expected. But at last Jugurtha was betrayed to him by one of his own household, and then Marius ended the war and brought the king captive to Rome.

No sooner was this war over than another one broke out which threatened the Romans with such a terrible danger that they elected Marius consul a second time to meet this new enemy; and then they elected him a third time, and a fourth time, and at last he was consul five times before the danger was past. It began to look as if the old prophecy would come true.

This new war was with a fierce and numerous people who came from the northeast and overran Gaul and threatened to pass over into Italy. They were called by several names, but they were probably Germans, and belonged to the same family of nations from which the Germans of to-day, the English, and most of the Americans are descended. They had large, strong bodies, and fierce blue eyes, and they terrified the Romans more even than the Gauls had done two hundred and eighty years before. Like the Gauls, they came in great numbers, carrying their wives and children and all their possessions with them in rude, covered wagons, and wandered about looking for a new home in which to settle.

The Romans first met these new-comers in that part of Gaul which had come under Roman rule. There four great armies of the Romans were destroyed one after the other. Then it was that Marius was elected consul a second time, and sent into Gaul to take the command and keep these Germans from crossing the Alps and coming into Italy.

Fortunately for the Romans, the barbarians turned aside into Spain after their last great victory, and wandered about in that country for two or three years. Thus Marius had time to get together a new army, and to drill his men and make them good soldiers. When the barbarians came back from Spain, they separated and one band of them started to go north around the Alps and enter Italy from the east, while the others remained in Gaul, and tried to enter the peninsula from the western side.

Even after so large a part of the Germans had left Gaul, Marius did not dare to lead his men out of camp against those that remained. For six days he let them march continuously past his camp; and as they went by they shouted taunts to the Romans and asked whether they had any messages to send to their wives. Then when the last of this band, too, had disappeared, Marius led his army out, and followed after them.

He came up with them just before they reached the Alps. By this time Marius had his soldiers so well trained that he decided to risk a battle. The result was a great victory for the Romans; for this band of the barbarians was entirely destroyed, and their kings were made captives.

Then Marius hurried on into Italy and marched to the aid of the other consul, who had been sent to meet the band who were seeking to enter the peninsula from the east. This consul was not so good a general as Marius, so the barbarians succeeded in getting into Italy on that side. When Marius arrived, they sent to him and demanded lands in Italy on which they and their brethren, whom they had left in Gaul, might settle. Then Marius showed them the captives who had been taken there, and said:

"Do not trouble yourselves for your brethren, for we have already provided lands for them which they shall possess forever."

Then the Germans were filled with grief and with anger, for they knew that their brethren had been destroyed. But the chiefs of their army challenged Marius to fix the time and place for a battle; and Marius named the third day after that for the day, and a broad plain near by for the place. When the battle came, the Germans fought with great bravery, and their women, standing in the wagons, encouraged their husbands and brothers with fierce cries; but at last the Romans were victorious and this band also of the barbarians was destroyed.

After this Marius returned to Rome, and there he was received with great honor and rejoicing. And men called him the third founder of the city; for, they said, just as Camillus saved Rome from the Gauls, so Marius had saved it from these new invaders. And soon after he was elected consul for the sixth time.

If Marius had been a statesman as well as a soldier, he might now have used his power to remedy the evils which the Gracchi had tried to cure, and so have saved the state. But though Marius could win battles, he could not rule the state in time of peace. Long after this, men said of him that "he never cared to be a good man, so he was a great one;" and perhaps that is the reason he failed as a ruler. At any rate, Marius hesitated to take either the side of the common people, or of the nobles, for he wished only to do the thing that would benefit himself. In this way Marius lost the influence which he had gained by his victories; and for twelve years the conqueror of the Germans was despised and neglected by both parties.

At last civil war began between the party of the common people and the party of the nobles. The nobles had a famous general named Sulla to command their army; so the leaders of the common people chose Marius, although he was then nearly seventy years old, to be their general. Marius had long been jealous of Sulla, and besides he was eager to gain the seventh consulship that had been promised him, so he accepted the command. But at first the party of Sulla got the better of the party of Marius; and when Sulla marched on Rome, the city was taken by his army. This was the first time that Rome was ever captured by an army of its own citizens, but it was not to be the last time.

SULLA.

When Rome was taken by Sulla, Marius escaped with much difficulty. For many days he wandered about Italy with only a few companions. At one time they barely escaped a party of horsemen on the shore by swimming out to some ships which were sailing by. At another time they lay hid in a marsh with the mud and water up to their necks. Once Marius was taken prisoner and the officers of the town where he was imprisoned sent a Gaulish slave to kill him in his dungeon; but Marius's eyes gleamed so fiercely in the darkness as he called out in a loud voice, "Fellow, darest thou kill Caius Marius?" that the slave dropped his sword and fled. Then the officers of the town were ashamed, and they let Marius go; and he escaped to Carthage in Africa. But even there he was not safe, for the Roman governor of that district sent men to warn him to leave; and when the men had told their message, Marius replied: "Go, tell the governor that you have seen Caius Marius sitting in exile among the ruins of Carthage."

At last Sulla was obliged to leave Italy and go to Asia Minor to make war on a powerful king who had arisen there. Then the friends of Marius got control of Rome once more; and Marius could safely return. When he came back his heart was filled with bitterness against his enemies, and he caused thousands of them to be put to death without trial or hearing; and even his friends came to fear this gloomy and revengeful old man.

At this time Marius gained his seventh consulship; but he did not live long to enjoy it. He fell into strange ways, and could not sleep at night; perhaps his conscience was troubling him for all the suffering he had caused. At last he died, on the seventeenth day of his seventh consulship; and all the world breathed freer when he was gone.

But soon Sulla returned from the East, and when he had regained his power he took a terrible revenge on all the friends of Marius. Many persons were put to death only because some one of Sulla's friends desired their goods. And the Italian cities which had rebelled against Rome in this time of trouble were punished with great severity; and so terribly was Italy wasted that it seemed as if Hannibal had come again.

XXIII

Cicero, the Orator.

AT the time that the war with Jugurtha was coming to an end, a boy was born at Marius's old home near Rome, who was to become as famous as Marius, but in a better and nobler way. He was to be a great orator and writer, and rule the state by his speaking as others ruled it by force of arms. As it takes more training to be great in this way than it does to be great as a soldier, perhaps you would like to hear how this boy was educated for his task. We will start with him as a tiny baby and follow him until he is a grown man.

First of all came the naming of the boy. This always took place on the eighth day after its birth, if the baby was a girl, but on the ninth day if the baby was a boy. So on the ninth day our baby was named, and he was given the name of his father and called "Marcus Tullius Cicero." The day was made a day of rejoicing in the family, and little gifts were hung about the baby's neck for him to play with.

After that the little fellow grew as most babies grow, and in time he learned to walk, and to talk in childish Latin. Perhaps, too, he began to speak Greek, even this early, from listening to the talk of some old slave or nurse of that country,—for the Roman boys and girls of this time often learned Greek in their homes just as American children sometimes learn German.

During his earliest years it was the child's mother who had the most to do with his education, just as you have seen Cornelia training her children. From his mother the boy learned to be pure in heart, and to be saving, modest, brave, earnest and obedient; and stories were told him of his forefathers, and of the ancient heroes who had made Rome great because they possessed these virtues.

When he became a little older and did not need the care of his mother so much, the father also began to take part in the education of young Marcus. Often he would take the little fellow with him, as he walked about to see that the slaves were cultivating his fields properly; and when he went to the house of a friend, and even sometimes when he went to the Forum of the little town where he lived, he would let the boy go with him. He taught the boy, too, manly exercises such as wrestling, riding and swimming. And when prayers were said to the gods by the father, and when sacrifices were offered on the family altar, the little boy stood by, or perhaps took some part in them; and so he learned about the gods that the Romans worshiped.

When Marcus Cicero became six or seven years old, it was time for him to begin to go to school. Because the schools in Rome were better than the schools in the country town where his parents lived, the boy was now taken to Rome to live with his uncle's family, and to go to school with his cousins.

The Roman schools were very different from the schools you go to. They began at sunrise, and in order not to be tardy the children had to be up and ready before daybreak. They carried lanterns with them to light their way, and slaves went with them to and from school to see that no harm befell them.

In the schoolroom, the schoolmaster sat on a raised platform at one end of the room, while the boys and girls sat on stools and benches in front of him. Around the walls there were lyres, or harps, to be used in the

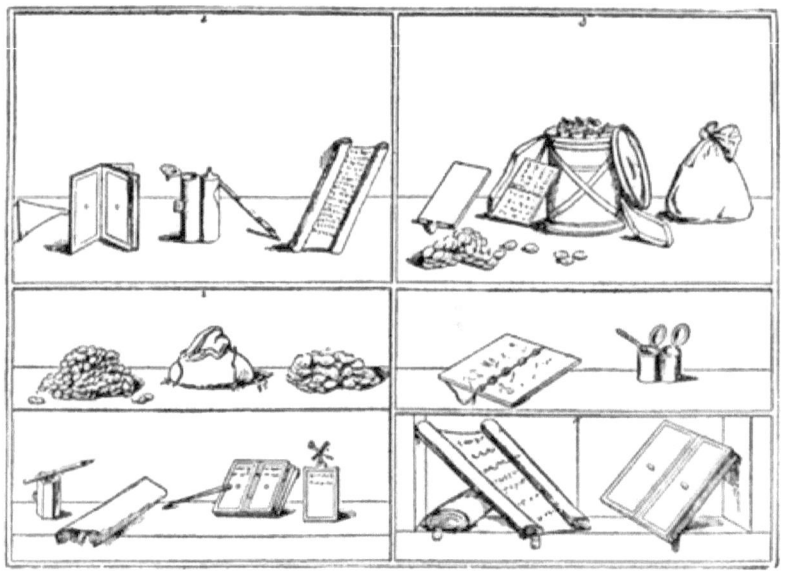

ROMAN BOOKS AND WRITING MATERIALS.

In two of the pictures purses and heaps of coins are also shown.

music lessons, and also pictures of the gods or of scenes from the history of Rome. On one of the walls a board was hung on which were written the names of all absent or truant pupils. Above the master's bench there was a great stick, and many of the boys looked tremblingly at it when they did not know their lessons.

In this lowest school, the children learned to read and to write. Instead of slates or sheets of paper, they had wooden tablets covered with wax; and on these they wrote with a sharp-pointed instrument called a stylus. The other end of the stylus was blunt, so that when a pupil made a mistake in his writing, he could smooth it out in the soft wax with this end, and then try again.

Here the children also learned arithmetic. Perhaps you think that the arithmetic which you have to learn is hard; but think how much harder it must have been for the Roman boys. They did not have the plain and easy figures which you use, but had only what we still call the "Roman numerals." If you want to see how much harder it is to use these, try to find the answer to

XXIV times LXXXVII,

and then see how much easier it is when it is written

24 times 87.

Because their arithmetic was so hard, each Roman boy carried with him to school a counting-frame to help him. This was a wooden frame divided into lines and columns, and he did his sums with it by putting little pebbles in the different columns to represent the different denominations.

After Cicero had passed out of this school, he went to what was called a grammar school. There he studied Greek grammar, and read some of the famous books of that day, both Greek and Latin. Of course these were not printed books, for printing was not invented till fifteen hundred years after this. The books of that time were all written with a pen, on smooth white skins' called parchment, or on paper made from the papyrus plant which grows in Egypt; and instead of being bound as our books are, the pages of these books were all pasted into one long strip, side by side, and then rolled tightly around a stick.

In this school young Cicero studied until he was fifteen years old. When a Roman boy became fifteen or sixteen years old, a great change usually came in his life. Up to that time he wore the "boyish toga," with its narrow purple border, and carried a "bulla" or charm about his neck to ward off the evil eye. After he passed that age, he put off the boyish toga and the bulla, and put on for the first time a toga all of white, such as the men wore. This, too, was made a day of festival, and after the change was made, the young man went with his father and his friends into the Forum, and there his name was written in the list of Roman citizens. After this he might be called upon to serve in war, and he had the right to vote and to do anything that the grown men were allowed to do. This was the change which came to Marcus Cicero when he was fifteen; and you can imagine how proud he felt as he went with his father from the Forum to the temples on the Capitol to offer sacrifices to the gods in honor of the day.

All Roman boys of good families followed the course of training which you have been reading about, up to the time when they put on the manly toga. After that, if they intended to train themselves for war, they entered the camp of some general and attached themselves to him; but if they intended to train themselves for the law, and become speakers, they attended the law courts in the Forum. Cicero's father wished him to be trained for the law, so he put the lad in charge of one of the great judges and lawyers of that time. In his company and under his direction, Cicero attended the law courts day after day, and listened to the best speakers, and took notes on all that he saw and heard. In this way he came, in the course of time, to know the laws of his country and the ways in which the courts did business; and by constant attention and practice, he also came to be a good speaker.

After a number of years spent in this way, Cicero at last had a chance to show the Roman people what good use he had made of his time in the law courts. During the terrible civil war between Marius and Sulla, a young Roman was charged most unjustly with the murder of his father, but all the lawyers of Rome were afraid to defend him, for it was known that whoever did so might anger Sulla, who was then ruling Rome, and so bring a sentence of death on himself. Cicero, however, was willing to risk the danger. He defended the young man before the court, and the cause was so good, and Cicero spoke so well and fearlessly in his defense, that the young man was at once released. This gave Cicero a good deal of fame at Rome; but he did not dare to remain there after that, for fear of the wrath of Sulla. So he went to Greece, and there he passed his time in studying under Greek masters, and learning how to speak and to write still better.

At last news came that Sulla was dead, and Cicero returned to Rome. Then he entered politics; and though the nobles looked upon him with scorn because he was a man of low birth—that is, because none of his family had ever held the office of consul at Rome—Cicero was such a good speaker, and so learned in the laws, and so honest, that he was elected to one office after another at the very lowest age that he could hold them.

Though he now held public offices, Cicero did not cease to come before the law courts whenever there was need. At one time a man named Verres was charged with greatly abusing the people of Sicily and unlawfully taking great sums of money from them while he was governor in that island. This had come to be a very common thing; indeed, people would often say that a Roman governor had to make three fortunes out of his province during the time that he was in office: one to pay off the debts he had made to get the office, another to bribe the judges at Rome in case they should try to punish him for his dishonesty, and a third to live on after he returned to Rome. So, although Verres was much worse than governors usually were, few people expected to see him punished. But Cicero took hold of the case, and he managed it so skilfully that in spite of all Verres could do he was forced to leave Rome and go into exile. This won for Cicero the praise of all honest citizens, but it is believed that it did not make the Roman governors very much better.

When Cicero had held all of the offices below that of consul, it happened that a plot was made at Rome which nearly overturned the government, and to prevent this from succeeding, Cicero was elected consul.

CICERO, THE ORATOR. 183

The common people and the nobles had by this time again begun their quarrels, which had been stopped during the time of Sulla's stern rule. A ruined noble, named Catiline, now put himself forward as the leader of the common people, and with their support he tried to gain the consulship. But all good men distrusted him, because of the crimes which were charged against him and because it was known that he was deeply in

CICERO.

debt and ready to do anything to get money. So the moderate men among both the common people and the nobles united in supporting Cicero for consul against Catiline, and Cicero was elected.

Then Catiline determined to secure by force what he could not get by the vote of the people. He got together a number of ruined nobles like himself, and planned to murder the consuls and then seize the city and burn and rob as they chose.

Cicero got news of these plans; but he did not dare to arrest Catiline, for he had powerful friends and Cicero did not yet have clear proof of the plot. He decided to try to anger and frighten Catiline so that he would openly show his plans and all people would be convinced of them. Accordingly, Cicero got up in the Senate, while Catiline was there, and made a powerful speech against him.

"How long, Catiline," he cried, "will you abuse our patience? When will this boldness of yours come to an end? Do not the guards which are placed each night on the Palatine hill alarm you? Do not the watchmen posted throughout the city, does not the alarm of the people and the union of all good men, do not the looks and expressions of the Senators here, have any effect upon you? Do you not feel that your plans are known? What did you do last night or the night before that you think is still unknown to us? or where did you meet, and who were there, and what plans did you adopt, that we do not know?"

Then Cicero went on to tell all the plans of Catiline, and showed him that so much was known of them that Catiline, in fright and rage, got up and left the temple in which the Senate was at that time meeting, and rode hastily away from the city to join some soldiers that he had raised. Then every one was sure that what Cicero had said about Catiline was true. An army was sent against the troops of Catiline, and they were easily overcome and Catiline was slain; and his followers in the city were arrested and put to death.

For Cicero's wise government of Rome at this time men of both parties honored him, and he was publicly called "the father of his country." But it was not long before the influence which he had gained in this way was greatly weakened.

Rome had grown, as you have seen, from a little city-state, to be a great empire; but the form of the government was still the same that it had been in the old days. This was bad, for a great empire cannot be ruled in the same way that a single city can. It was not only unjust, but it was unwise to let a few thousand greedy, selfish men at Rome choose the officers and make the laws that were to rule all the millions of people that were governed by Rome. But nobody knew the true way to remedy the trouble, for nobody had then thought of what we call "representative government,"—that is, a government in which the people of each city or district elect men to represent them at the capital of the country, and make laws for the whole land. The Romans knew only two ways of governing a great empire: one was to let the people of the chief city rule over all the rest as Rome was doing; the other was to give up free government altogether, and let a king or despot rule over the whole according to his will.

Many people thought that the government by the Senate and people of Rome could still be kept up. Cicero was one of these, and he tried to build up a party in support of this idea. But the task was too great. The Senators were selfish and short-sighted; the rich men were greedy and corrupt; and the common people were ready to support any one who would only give them bread to eat and amuse them with circus races and wild-beast fights. Besides this, several powerful men had now arisen, each of whom was trying to make himself master of Rome.

So Cicero failed in his task. First he was exiled from Rome, on a charge of unlawfully punishing some of the followers of Catiline. Then, after he had been allowed to return to Rome, civil war broke out between

CIRCUS MAXIMUS.

the different men who were trying to get the chief power; and the wars continued until at last the Republic came to an end, and Julius Cæsar—whose story you will read in the next two chapters—gathered up all the offices of the government in his own hands, and made himself sole ruler of the whole Roman empire.

In this time of terrible civil war, Cicero could have no place, for he was a peaceful man who tried to rule men by persuading them, instead of commanding them by force. And after the old government had been overthrown, he no longer took an interest in politics. After that, he spent his time in studying and writing; and the books which he wrote at this time may still be read by those who understand the Latin language,— indeed, it is not too much to say, that they have done more to make the name of Cicero famous than anything else that he ever did.

But before many years had passed in this way, Cæsar was slain by some of his enemies, and new struggles began for the mastery of the Roman world. Cicero now thought that perhaps the government by the Senate and people might be restored, and he spoke and wrote in order to bring this about. But it was in vain. The attempt to restore the old government failed, and Cicero lost his own life by it. His writings had angered some of the great men of Rome, and at last they ordered that he should be put to death.

The soldiers who were sent to carry out the order found Cicero at his pleasant country home by the sea. His faithful slaves wished to defend him against the soldiers, but Cicero knew that this could not save him; so he commanded them not to resist the soldiers, and then calmly submitted to his fate.

Long after this, one of the men who had given the order for Cicero's death, found his nephew with a book in his hand, which the boy tried to hide under his gown. He took the book from the boy's hand, and then saw that it was one of Cicero's works. For a long time he stood and read in the book; then, as he gave it back to him, he cried:

"My child, this was a learned man, and one who loved his country well."

XXIV

Julius Cæsar, the Conqueror of Gaul.

CAIUS JULIUS CÆSAR belonged to a noble family, but he was a nephew of Marius by marriage, and it was this perhaps that caused him first to act with the party of the people.

He was little more than a boy when the parties of Sulla and Marius were carrying on their terrible struggles for the mastery, and he had taken no part in these troubles. But when Sulla had overcome the party of Marius, and was putting to death all persons whom he regarded as the enemies of his own party, he wished to include young Cæsar in the number. The Vestal Virgins, however, and some of Sulla's firmest friends, went to him and begged that Cæsar's life might be spared, because of his youth and his noble birth. For a long time they pleaded in vain, but at last Sulla gave way.

"Let him be spared, then, as you wish," he said; "but I would have you know that there is many a Marius in this young man, for whose safety you are so anxious; and you will find, some day, that he will be the ruin of the party of the nobles to which you and I all belong."

After this narrow escape Cæsar did not dare to stay longer at Rome. He went to the lands about the eastern end of the Mediterranean Sea, and joined the camp of a Roman general who was carrying on one of the wars, which the Romans were now waging nearly all the time in that region. Here Cæsar got his first training in war; and one day he showed such bravery in saving the life of a fellow soldier, that the general in command of the army presented him with a crown of oak leaves. This, as you will remember from the story of Coriolanus, was a great mark of honor among the Romans.

After Sulla was dead, Cæsar returned to Rome; but he did not remain there long. He decided that he wanted to be an orator as well as a soldier, so he went to Greece, as Cicero had done, to study the art of writing and speaking.

While Cæsar was on his way to Greece, he had an adventure which shows very well the sort of man that he was. The ship that he was on was captured by pirates, and Cæsar was told by them that he must pay a large sum of money before they would let him go. He at once sent his servants to raise this sum, but in the meantime he had to stay with the pirates at their island home.

They were desperate men, who considered the crime of murder a trifling act; but Cæsar seemed to have no fear of them, and even showed his contempt for them quite freely. When he wished to sleep, he would order them to be silent while he did so; at other times he would join in their rough play and exercise. To help pass away the time till his servants should return, he wrote poems and speeches, and spoke them to these ignorant men; and when they did not show pleasure in what he recited he frankly called them "dunces" and "barbarians." They took all this from Cæsar with great good-humor, for they liked his fearless spirit; and when he threatened to punish them, as soon as he was free, for their piracy and crimes, they laughed and thought this a great joke.

When his money had come, however, and he was set free, the first thing that Cæsar did was to carry out this threat. He gathered together some ships and men, and returned to the island where the pirates stayed. He found their vessels still at anchor there, and in the battle which followed, he not only defeated and captured most of the men, but also recovered the money which he had paid them as a ransom.

At Rome, Cæsar led the same sort of life that other wealthy young Romans did at that time. He joined in the gayety of the city, and seemed to think of nothing but that. He was very careful in his dress, and was one of the leaders of the fashion at Rome. This seemed foolish to the grave Cicero, and he once spoke doubtfully of Cæsar, wondering if there could really be any earnest purpose in a man who gave so much thought to the arrangement of his hair.

But this was only the outside view of Cæsar. He had already set his heart on doing something great, so as to make his name remembered; and he never forgot this purpose. At the very time that Cicero thought him so foolish and careless, Cæsar was preparing himself to win the favor of the people and become their leader. When he began to speak in public, he had taken so much pains to train himself well, that he pleased his hearers from the first; and after his return from Greece, he was looked upon as one of the best orators of Rome. He was friendly and pleasant to every one, and gave money freely to all who asked for it. In this way he won the favor of the people, and soon he was elected to several offices, one after the other.

While Cæsar held one of these offices, it was his duty to oversee the public games. The Romans, as you know, had now become very fond of such shows, and they were given a number of times each year. There were many kinds of these games. Some of them were like the Greek games, and were contests in running, wrestling, leaping, and hurling the spear. Others were sham battles, in which little armies of horsemen, infantry, and elephants took part. But the kinds that the Romans liked best were three,—the chariot races, the fights with wild beasts, and the contests of gladiators.

The chariot races were held in a race course called the Great Circus, which lay between the Palatine hill and the hill which stood south of it. Each chariot was usually drawn by four horses, and four chariots took part in each race. The driver of each chariot wore a different colored gown,—one white, one red, one blue, and one green; and the people took such interest in these races, that they divided into parties over them. In this way there arose a party of the Greens, who always favored the driver who wore that color, and a party of the Blues, who favored the one in blue, and so on; and sometimes the people became so excited by the races that the different parties actually came to blows about them.

The chariot races were very old,—indeed, it was said that Romulus first started them; but the wild-beast fights were not introduced until after the second war with Carthage. Then the Romans began to turn loose elephants, lions, leopards, and other beasts, in the "arena" of the Circus (as the central part of it was called), and set men to hunt them for the amusement of the spectators. In this way four hundred lions were once turned loose at the same time.

But the shows which the people liked best of all were the fights of the gladiators. The gladiators were men who were trained to fight to amuse the Romans; and

CHARIOT RACE.

they were usually captives who had been taken in war, or slaves who had been sold to the trainers of gladiators as a punishment. Most often they fought together in single pairs. Sometimes they were both armed in the same way, with helmet, shield, and sword. Sometimes, however, one only would be armed in this way, and the other would have nothing but a three-pointed spear with which to thrust at his enemy, and a net to throw over his head and entangle him. When one of the gladiators became wounded, the fight stopped until the will of the people had been made known. If they held their thumbs up, he was spared; but if they turned their thumbs so that they pointed downward, he was at once put to death.

GLADIATOR FIGHT.

The government was supposed to furnish the money to provide for these games, but the custom had arisen for the overseers of the games to add to them at their own expense. So when Cæsar was overseer he determined to furnish finer games than had ever been seen before. In this he succeeded. Everybody said that there had never been more or better gladiator fights or finer wild-beast hunts than those he furnished. The statues and pictures, too, which he provided to decorate the Forum and the temples on the Capitol, during the time that the games were being held, were so numerous that places had to be found elsewhere to exhibit many of them.

Cæsar spent such large sums of his own money on these shows that he came out of the office very heavily in debt; but he had succeeded in his purpose. He had made the people think him generous and public-spirited; so when he became a candidate for the consulship some time after this, they gladly supported him. The nobles, however, did not like Cæsar so well, and they opposed his election, for they were already beginning to fear his power over the people. But at this time there was a powerful man at Rome who could help Cæsar very much with his election, if he would, and he needed Cæsar's help as much as Cæsar needed his.

This man was named Pompey, and he was called "the Great" because of his deeds in war. At one time he had put down a dangerous rebellion in Spain. After that he had helped to put down a rebellion of gladiators, who had fled in large numbers to Mount Vesuvius in Italy, and formed a strong camp there. Then, some time after Cæsar's adventure with the pirates, Pompey had been given a great fleet and had been commissioned to make war on the pirates. With this fleet he had started in at the Straits of Gibraltar, and searched every nook and corner of the Mediterranean Sea, and swept all the pirates before him till he reached the coast of Asia; there he defeated them in one great battle, and so cleared the seas of pirates for many years. After that, Pompey had been given the command in a war with a king who ruled on the southern shore of the Black Sea; and in this war also he had been successful. So at last Pompey had come back to Rome with much honor, and was given a great triumph by the people; but the nobles looked upon him with suspicion, and refused to reward his soldiers, and to approve the arrangements which he had made for the conquered country in the East.

This vexed Pompey very much; so he joined with Cæsar, and they agreed to help each other in gaining what they each wanted. In this way Pompey got lands for his soldiers and had his acts in the East approved; and Cæsar got his election as consul. After his year as consul was up, and it was time for him to go as governor to one of the provinces, as was the custom, Cæsar was appointed governor of Gaul for five years. And before that time was up, by a new agreement between the two men, Cæsar was given another term of five years as governor of Gaul, while Pompey was appointed to govern Spain for an equal time.

The Senators were not sorry to see Cæsar go to Gaul, for they hoped that during his long absence from the city, the fickle people of Rome might forget him, and so leave him without influence when he returned; or, if this should not happen, they hoped at any rate that something might occur in the meantime to make his influence less dangerous to the party of the nobles.

At this time there were two districts which the Romans called by the name of Gaul, and Cæsar was given command over both of these. One was on the Italian side of the Alps, and included the lands in the valley of the River Po, on which those Gauls had lived who welcomed Hannibal when he came into Italy. This was called "Cis-Alpine Gaul," or "Gaul on this side of the Alps." The other lay on the other side of the Alps, in what is now southern France, and this was called "Trans-Alpine Gaul."

Cis-Alpine Gaul had been conquered for some time, but in Trans-Alpine Gaul the power of the Romans did not extend beyond a little strip of land in the southern part, where the country touches the Mediterranean Sea. Moreover, the affairs of Gaul beyond the Alps had been neglected by the Romans during the struggles that had taken place at Rome, and when Cæsar reached his provinces he found that troubles were beginning there which needed his immediate attention.

Cæsar learned that a large body of people who lived in the valleys of the Alps, had determined to leave their homes among the mountains, and search out new ones in the western part of Gaul. They had burned their towns and villages, so that their people could have no wish to return to their old homes, and they were now ready to start on their journey through the Roman province, carrying their families and their goods with them.

The march of so large a body of the Swiss through Trans-Alpine Gaul might mean the beginning of much trouble for the Romans; so Cæsar determined that they must be stopped before they had gone any farther from their homes. He crossed the Alps in haste, therefore, and sent word to the Swiss forbidding them to march through his province. Then, when they tried in spite of this to force their way out of the mountains, he defeated them in a terrible battle; and sent them back to their own country, to rebuild their burned homes and settle upon their own lands once more.

This great victory gave Cæsar's soldiers confidence in their new commander; and it also caused many of the neighboring tribes of Gaul to submit to him, and become friends to the Roman people.

Soon after this the chiefs of one of these tribes appealed to Cæsar for aid in a trouble of their own; and begged him to help them against a tribe of Germans, who had lately crossed the Rhine, and come into Gaul. These Germans had already conquered a part of the country, and were inviting other German tribes to cross the river and join them in overrunning the whole of Gaul. This would have been more dangerous even than to have had the Swiss passing through the country in search of new homes; so Cæsar determined to give the help that was asked of him, and send the Germans also back to their own lands.

But while Cæsar was preparing to march against the Germans, his army began to give him trouble. The Gauls and the Roman traders who passed through the camp, told marvelous tales of the great size of the Germans, and of the fierceness of their appearance, and of their skill with their weapons. When Cæsar's soldiers heard these stories, and when it was whispered among them that they were about to march against the Germans, they began to fear this people as much as Marius's soldiers had done before them. Some of the young officers, who had had little experience in war, even began to make excuses to be allowed to return to Rome; others, who were ashamed to leave the army in this way, made their wills, and went about the camp with tears streaming down their faces. These claimed that it was not the enemy they feared; but that they dreaded the narrowness of the roads, and the vastness of the forests through which the men would have to pass, and they were afraid, too, that there would not be food enough for the army on its march.

When Cæsar heard these things, he called a meeting of his soldiers and rebuked them.

"Is it your business," he asked, "to inquire in what direction we are to march, and what are the plans of your general? Is it your duty to think of the feeding of the army, and the condition of the roads? That is my affair, and not yours; and you should not distrust me so much as to think that I will not attend to it. I suspect, indeed, that it is the enemy that you dread, and not the dangers of the march. But even though you know that you are to fight against the Germans, what is it that you fear in them? They have already been defeated by Marius within the memory of our fathers. The Swiss, whom you have so lately sent back to their homes, have defeated them in their own country. Shall we not be able to do what they have succeeded in doing? I had intended to put off this march of ours to a more distant day; but now I have determined to break up our camp during this very night, so that I may find out as soon as possible whether my soldiers will answer to the call of duty, or give way to fear. If no others will follow me, I shall still go forward with the tenth legion alone; for I know that the men of that legion, at least, are too brave ever to desert their commander."

On hearing these words, the minds of the soldiers were suddenly changed. The tenth legion sent messengers to him to thank him for his confidence in them;

and the soldiers of the other legions made excuses for themselves, and begged him to believe that they would follow him wherever he might wish to go. Cæsar accepted their excuses; but that night, as he had said he would, he began the march. And when the army came up with the Germans, and a battle was fought, Cæsar easily defeated the enemy and drove them back across the Rhine into their own country.

These two wars were the beginning of Cæsar's command in Gaul. In a few months, he had succeeded in saving the country from being overrun by the Swiss and by the Germans; and perhaps he had even kept the barbarians from entering Italy again as in the time of Marius. He remained governor of Gaul for nine years in all, and during that time he conquered all the country from the Rhine west to the Atlantic Ocean, and from the Roman province in the south to the English Channel on the north. He did even more than this. Twice when he wished to overawe the restless tribes of Germany, he quickly built a bridge over the wide and rapid stream of the Rhine, and led his army over to frighten the neighboring tribes into submission; and twice, also, he gathered ships and crossed over into the neighboring island of Great Britain, to make war upon the tribes that lived there and punish them for having interfered in the affairs of Gaul.

Cæsar was the first Roman general to lead an army into either Germany or Britain; and although he made no serious attempt to subdue these countries himself, he prepared the way for the conquest of Britain, at least, in the time that was to come. In Gaul, however, he completely conquered the country. When he left that land its people had already settled down quietly under the Roman rule, and they were beginning to learn the Roman customs and the Roman language. So thoroughly did they learn these that they became almost like the Romans themselves, and even to-day the language that is spoken in that land—the French language—is merely a form of the old Latin tongue, which their Roman conquerors spoke nearly two thousand years ago.

One of the things that helped Cæsar most in this great work of conquest, was his power over the common soldiers. During all the years that they fought under him in Gaul, they never once repeated the threat of disobedience, which they had made when he first proposed to lead them against the Germans. From that time on they were entirely devoted to him, for they had confidence in him. He was willing to share every danger and hardship with his soldiers, and when he made a speech to them he called them "Fellow soldiers," to show that he was one of them. In the marches with his army, he used to go at the head of his troops, sometimes on horseback, but oftener on foot, with his head bare in all kinds of weather. At the beginning of a battle, he often sent his horse away, so that he might lead his men on foot. If they began to give way during the fight he would go among them and stop those that were flying, and turn them towards the enemy again; and so by courage and determination he would change defeat into victory.

Cæsar was both mild and strict in his control of his men. After they had won the victory he would allow them to rest and make merry; but before the battle had been fought and the victory decided, he demanded unceasing watchfulness and entire obedience. He would give no notice of battle till the last moment, in order that the soldiers might always hold themselves in readiness for it; and, for the same reason, he would often lead his men out of their camp, when there was no need of it, even in rainy weather and on holidays. Sometimes, either by day or night, he would suddenly give them orders to follow without losing sight of him; and then lead them on long marches in order to test their strength, and to prepare them for doing the same thing whenever there might be real necessity for it. In this way, long before Cæsar's nine years in Gaul were over, he had an army of veterans, every man of whom was willing to follow him into any danger.

While Cæsar was still in Gaul, he wrote the account of his struggles with the barbarians, and sent it to Rome, so that the people might know of the successes of his army. Many of the Roman books have been lost, but this account of Cæsar's wars in Gaul is so well written and so interesting that it was carefully saved, and if you should ever study Latin, this will be almost the first book that you will read.

XXV

Cæsar and the Beginning of the Empire.

DURING the years of Cæsar's life in Gaul, the misgovernment of Rome had steadily been growing worse. The elections for consuls could not be held without disorder, and the candidates for office went about with bands of armed men for their protection. Sometimes these bands actually fought at the voting places; and once the election of consuls was prevented, by these quarrels, for six months after the proper time. Thus the Romans were not only failing to rule their provinces justly,—as you have seen was so in the case of Verres in Sicily,—but the city itself was now filled with confusion and violence; and many wise and thoughtful men became willing to end the disorder in any way that was possible.

At this time, Cicero was trying to cure the evils of the government by urging the people of Rome to be as unselfish and virtuous as their forefathers had been. His efforts failed, for the people were not willing to believe that their greed and selfishness were ruining their country; and, perhaps, if they had believed it, they could not have changed themselves in order to make their government better. They had no idea of reforming the government by giving it the representative form such as we have now; so the only cure that remained was for the government by the

Senate to give way to that of one strong man, who could put down disorder and punish misgovernment.

But where was the strong man to be found who could, and would, force the Senate to step aside and let him carry on the government? To do this, it was necessary that he should have an army, for the Senate would certainly not give up its power without a struggle. Now there were only two men at this time who had armies which they could use in this way. One of them was Pompey, the conqueror of the pirates and the East; the other was Cæsar, the conqueror of Gaul.

Pompey might long ago have overturned the government of the Senate, if he had really wanted to do so. But though he could win battles, he did not know much about government, and could not make up his mind what he wanted to do. Cæsar, on the other hand, was as good at politics as he was at war. He had long seen that the old government was so bad that it could only be cured by setting up another in its place; and he was quite ready to try to do this himself, if the chance should come to him.

For a while Cæsar and Pompey had acted together, and had helped each other in politics. But when news came to Pompey at Rome of the splendid victories which Cæsar was winning in Gaul, he began to be jealous of him, and at last he was ready to join with the party of the nobles in any plan that would destroy Cæsar's power.

As you will remember, it had been agreed that Cæsar was to have his command in Gaul for ten years. When that time should be up, he had arranged that he should be elected consul again. That would give him an army as consul, just as soon as he laid down the command of his army in Gaul; and when his year as consul was up, he would go to one of the provinces as the head of another army for a long term of years. In this way there would be no time when Cæsar would not have an army at his command; and so the nobles would not be able to injure him, or put him to death, as they had put Tiberius and Caius Gracchus to death.

The plan which the nobles and Pompey formed, to get rid of Cæsar, was this. They would make him give up his government in Gaul before his last five years were over; then, perhaps, when Cæsar had no army to protect him against injustice, they would bring him to trial before the courts at Rome on some charge—any charge would do—and have him convicted. In this way they would get rid of him, and the selfish government of the Senate could go on as before.

To carry out this plan, the Senate ordered Cæsar to give up his governorship, and return to Rome. Cæsar knew that he could not trust himself there without an army to protect him; still, he made an offer to the Senate to give up his command, if Pompey, who was then at Rome with an army near by, would give up his command also. The Senate replied that Cæsar must give up his army, or become a traitor to his country; and that Pompey need not give up his.

Cæsar now saw that his enemies were planning to destroy him; but to resist them meant the beginning of a civil war between himself and Pompey. Nevertheless, he prepared to lead his victorious army across the little river Rubicon, which separated Cis-Alpine Gaul from Italy, and march south to attack his enemies.

The old stories say that after Cæsar had drawn up his men on the banks of the river he stood for some time in deep thought, questioning whether it was the wisest thing, after all, for him to go in arms against the government of his country. While he stood in doubt, a wandering minstrel near by suddenly seized a trumpet from one of the soldiers and sounded the call to advance. Cæsar took this as a sign from the gods, and exclaimed:

"Let us go whither the gods and the wickedness of our enemies call us. The die is now cast."

Then he led his veteran soldiers across the Rubicon and marched south to meet the army of Pompey.

Pompey meanwhile had made almost no preparations for the war.

ROMAN SOLDIERS.

When some one had asked him what he would do if Cæsar should march into Italy, Pompey had replied:

"I have but to stamp my foot, and soldiers will spring up all over Italy to fill the legions of my army."

But after Cæsar had crossed the Rubicon, news was soon brought to Rome that the Italian towns were yielding to him without a struggle; and when one of the Senators taunted Pompey with his vain boast, and asked him why he did not stamp his foot, the latter could find no answer. It was too late now to raise men to save Rome; so Pompey had to leave the city to its fate. He retreated with his army to the south of Italy; but Cæsar promptly followed him. Then, rather than to fight in Italy, Pompey crossed over into Greece; for his influence was strongest there and in the East, where his greatest victories had been won. Cæsar could now follow him no further, for some time for want of ships to carry his men across the sea.

Cæsar, accordingly, now turned back to Rome, having driven his enemies from Italy in sixty days, without the shedding of a drop of blood. At Rome he treated the people mildly and generously, and the men who had feared that the terrible times of Sulla and Marius had come again, soon saw that they were mistaken. Cæsar punished no one, and he took the property of none. He remained in the city only a short time, and then, although Pompey himself had gone to the East, Cæsar set out for Spain, where the greatest part of Pompey's army had been left.

"I go," he said, "to attack an army without a general; I shall return to attack a general without an army."

After some difficulty, Cæsar succeeded in getting possession of the Roman provinces in Spain. He now had Gaul, Italy and Spain under his control, and he could turn all his efforts against Pompey and the forces in the East.

He now led his army back through Italy by rapid marches; and, although it was by this time the middle of winter, he immediately crossed into Greece. Then, for about four months, the two armies marched and countermarched, and built camps and threw up earthworks. During all this time Pompey's army was larger than Cæsar's; and it was better fed and better cared for also, as Pompey's ships could bring him everything that he needed, while Cæsar's men had to live off the country around them. For a long time Cæsar tried to bring on a battle, but without success; for Pompey knew that though he had the larger number of men, Cæsar had the better soldiers. At last, however, Pompey yielded to the urging and flattery of his followers, and drew out his men for battle. The result was a great victory for Cæsar. Although Pompey had twice as many men as Cæsar had, he was defeated and his army was destroyed.

After this battle, Pompey was forced to fly from Greece and seek refuge in Egypt. There he was basely murdered by men who wished to please Cæsar, and thought that this would be the surest way of winning his favor. But when Cæsar followed Pompey to Egypt, and was shown the proofs of his death, he did not rejoice, but turned away his face and wept. To all the men who had been in Pompey's army, he showed himself kind and generous; and he wrote to his friends at Rome that "the chief pleasure he had in his victory was in saving every day some one of his fellow citizens who had borne arms against him."

After Cæsar's victory over Pompey, he established his power firmly in Greece, Egypt and Asia, as he had already done in the western part of the Mediterranean countries. When he returned to Rome, Africa was the only portion of the Roman Empire that remained unconquered; and all of Cæsar's enemies who were left had gathered there. For a time Cæsar remained at

Rome to attend to public affairs; but as soon as he could, he arranged to go to Africa and conquer this last army of his enemies.

But Cæsar's soldiers were wearied with marching from one end of the world to the other. The tenth legion, which had served him so long and well, at last rebelled, and the men demanded that they should be dismissed with the rewards that were due them for their long services. When Cæsar heard this, he went out to meet them, and said, coldly:

"Citizens, you shall be dismissed as you desire, and you shall have all the rewards which have been promised you."

When the soldiers heard their beloved commander call them "citizens," instead of "fellow soldiers," as always before, their minds were suddenly changed. They could not bear the cold disapproval which lay in that word. They begged that they might be taken back into his service again; and after that, there was no longer any talk of disobedience on their part.

Cæsar was as successful in defeating his enemies in Africa as he had been everywhere else, and when he returned to Rome, he was able to celebrate four triumphs, one after the other, for his victories in Gaul, in Egypt, in Asia, and in Africa. On the day of his triumph over Gaul, he ascended the Capitol at night, with twenty elephants carrying torches on his right hand, and twenty on his left. When he triumphed because of his victories in Asia, an inscription was carried before his chariot which read in Latin, "I came, I saw, I conquered"; this was copied from a message which Cæsar had sent to the Senate to announce one of his victories, and it was intended to remind the people how quickly he had ended the troubles in that region.

Cæsar was now master of Rome and of her empire. The Roman army, made up of men of all countries, was the strongest power in the state; and Cæsar, who controlled the army, was the first man in the empire. He could now make whatever reforms in the state he thought best. As the Senate and the people had

CÆSAR'S TRIUMPH.

shown so plainly that they were no longer fit for the task of governing the peoples under their rule, he decided to carry on the government himself. He allowed the Senate and the assemblies of the people to meet as before, but he took good care to see that they had no real power. He gathered most of the offices of the state into his own hands; and, besides the titles which went with these offices, he gave himself the name of "Emperor," or commander, and that in time came to be the highest title of all.

Cæsar used his great power well. Instead of treating those who had fought against him as Sulla and Marius had treated their enemies, he tried to make them his friends, and allowed them to hold offices under him. There were still some men left who were determined to defy him to the last, and these joined together in Spain under the sons of Pompey, and Cæsar was compelled to leave Rome, and lead the army against them himself before they were finally defeated. But the greater part of the people of Rome were satisfied with the rule of Cæsar, because it promised to give the peace and safety which they had not enjoyed for many years.

Cæsar lived for only two years after the four-fold triumph which followed his return from Africa. In those two years, however, he succeeded in doing much good for Rome. He made laws for the reform of the courts of justice, and others to enable men who were in debt, and could not pay, to settle with their creditors. He tried to reform the manners of life of the Romans by passing laws against extravagance in dress and in banquets. He tried to check the growth of slave labor by requiring that one-third of the laborers on sheep-farms must be free. He planned new colonies to provide for the poor and idle population of Rome; and he passed laws to admit many of the subjects of Rome to an equality with the citizens of the city itself.

Another of the reforms which he carried out is of especial interest to us, because the civilized world to-day still profits by it. This was the reform of the calendar. The Romans divided the year into twelve months, as we do; but their months were not long enough, so they had an awkward way of putting in an extra month about every two years, to make the seasons come out right. This plan worked badly, and, by the time of Cæsar, the calendar and the real year of the earth's revolution around the sun, had become ninety days apart. As a result of this, the Italian farmer began his work in the fields in June and July, according to the calendar, when it was really March and April. Cæsar consulted the most learned men of his time, and the calendar was corrected and made to agree with the seasons. Then, to keep it right in the future, Cæsar increased the length of some of the months, so that the ordinary year should have three hundred and sixty-five days; and he arranged that every fourth year, or leap year, an extra day should be given to February. The calendar after this worked very well, and with one small change we use it to this day, with the Roman names for the months and all; and to keep in memory the part which Cæsar had in this reform, we still call one of the months "July" from his name, Julius.

Besides these various reforms, Cæsar planned many other important works. He planned to collect a large library at Rome, and this was at a time when books were very rare and costly. He was beginning a new theater, and planning to build a new Senate house, as the old one had been burned in the terrible disorders of the late wars. A great temple to Mars was to keep the memory of his victories fresh in the minds of the people.

At the mouth of the Tiber, an immense harbor was to be built, and a new road was to lead east through the mountains to the Adriatic Sea. And in the midst of all this he was preparing to lead armies against the barbarians on the Danube, and against those south of the Caspian Sea in Asia; for in both these regions the peoples were forcing their way out of their own lands and seeking to come into the Roman provinces.

But all these plans were left unfinished or were not even begun. Although Rome was now better off than it had been at any time for fifty years, there were some men among her citizens who still thought that there was nothing more shameful than to submit to the rule of one man. They longed for the old government of the Senate with all its faults. At last sixty of the nobles formed a plot to kill Cæsar, and so free themselves from his power in the only way that was possible. Almost all of these men had received favors from Cæsar, and one of them, Marcus Brutus, had been admitted to close friendship with him. But crafty and selfish men persuaded Brutus that it was his duty to his country to overthrow Cæsar, just as his ancestor had overthrown Tarquin long before. So Brutus joined the plot and became one of its leaders.

Cæsar was warned of the danger that threatened him, but he would have no guards about him.

"It is better to die once," he said, "than to live always in fear of death."

He had been warned especially to beware of the day which the Romans called the "Ides" of March; but on that day he went to the Senate house as usual. On the way there he saw the priest who had told him to beware of the day; and he laughed at him for a false prophet, because the ides of March had come and nothing had befallen him. But the priest answered:

"The day is come, Cæsar, but it is not yet gone."

When Cæsar entered the Senate house, all the Senators arose to greet him, as was their custom. Then the plotters advanced to Cæsar's chair, one of them pretending to beg a favor of him, while the rest appeared to urge Cæsar to grant this request.

Suddenly one of the plotters laid hold of Cæsar's toga, and dragged it from his shoulders. This was a signal for the others, and at once they fell upon Cæsar with their swords and daggers. For a moment Cæsar resisted them, but when he saw his friend Brutus striking at him among the number, he cried out:

"Thou, too, Brutus!"

With this he ceased his struggles; and wrapping his head in his toga, he fell, pierced with many wounds, at the foot of the statue of Pompey which stood in the Senate house.

Thus died one of the greatest men who ever lived in any country or at any time. There have been many men in the world who have been great in one way; but Cæsar was great in many ways. He was a better general, perhaps, than any man before or since his time; but he was more than this. He was a good writer and one of the best orators among the Romans. He was a wise ruler, who saw clearly what his country needed in many different lines, and who spent the short time during which he held the power in planning reforms and improvements for her benefit. But best of all, he had a generous and fearless spirit, and found it easy to forgive those who had injured him, and easier to die than to dread to die.

He was worthy to become, as he did, the first of a long line of Roman emperors. He has made his name, too, a word of honor in the world to this day; for when the Germans call their emperor "Kaiser," they merely give him Cæsar's name; and when the Russians speak of their ruler as the "Czar," they, too, are using the name of this great Roman.

XXVI

Rome in the Time of Augustus.

THE enemies of Cæsar were able to put him to death, but they could not bring back the Republic, which he had overthrown. After Cæsar was gone, the quarrels and struggles which he had brought to an end began once more. Cæsar had left no son to succeed him, but when his will was opened it was found that he had adopted his nephew Octavius as his son, and made him his heir.

Octavius was not yet nineteen years old, but he soon showed that he possessed wisdom which was beyond his years. He accepted the inheritance and set himself to work to secure his rights under it. After many difficulties, he succeeded in doing this. Then he set to work to secure the punishment of Cæsar's murderers. This required much time and care, on the part of Octavius; but at last they were defeated in battle and slain, and thus he succeeded in this also. Then he began to plan to secure Cæsar's power in the empire for himself, as Cæsar's successor. This was the hardest thing that he had yet attempted, for there were other men who were trying to get as much power as they could, and Octavius had to struggle against them. In the end, however, he succeeded in getting what he wanted. All of his rivals were got rid of, except one; then, twelve years after the death of

Cæsar, Octavius won a great battle over this man, and became master of the whole Roman world.

For a hundred years—ever since the time of the Gracchi—the party of the people and the party of the nobles had been struggling together, but neither one could find a cure for the troubles that filled the Roman lands. The world was now worn out with these struggles. The time had come when both the nobles and the people must finally yield to the rule of one man, with an army to carry out his commands. In this way alone could peace and order and happiness be brought to the millions of people who were under the Roman rule. Octavius established the rule of the empire, which Cæsar had begun; and he established it so firmly that it lasted undisturbed for five hundred years after him. From the time that Octavius got the power, there was no longer any question as to what form of government there should be; the only question was, who should be the one to carry on the government under the form of rule that he had set up.

When Octavius became emperor he took the name "Augustus," and it is by that name that we must now speak of him. He was a good ruler, and during the many years that he governed the empire, the world about the Mediterranean was happier than it had ever been before. The doors of the temple of Janus, which had been shut only three times since Rome was founded, were now closed again for long periods; for peace—"the Roman peace," as it was proudly called —was spread over the world. From Spain to Greece, from Gaul to Egypt, there was no longer any war. Travelers came and went in safety on the great roads

AUGUSTUS CÆSAR.

with which the Romans had covered the world; the farmers sowed and reaped their fields in peace, and the merchants sent out their goods by land and sea and had no cause to fear that an enemy might arise to rob them of their gains.

Augustus decided that the empire was now as large as it ought ever to become. He fixed the rivers Rhine and Danube as the boundaries, on the north, beyond which the Romans should not seek to rule; and he caused a chain of forts to be built along these rivers to defend the Roman lands against the attacks of the wild tribes who lived beyond. Nearly all the emperors who came after Augustus respected these limits. Almost the only land that was added to the empire after this time was the island of Britain,—and Julius Cæsar, you will remember, had already prepared the way for its conquest while he was conquering Gaul.

At Rome, Augustus had many new temples built, and many of the old ones, which were falling into decay, he caused to be repaired and covered over with a facing of marble. Before he died, he could say, in speaking of this work:

"I found Rome built of brick, but I leave it built of marble."

Augustus was also fond of encouraging and rewarding poets and other writers. Partly because of this there were more great literary men at Rome during this time than ever before or after; and for this reason whenever we wish to describe a period when literature flourished and great writers lived and wrote, we still call it an "Augustan age."

Let us now try to look, for a little while, into the life

TOGA—FRONT.

TOGA—BACK.

of the city in this happy time while it was under the wise rule of Augustus. Of course, we shall want to see something of these great Roman authors, so we will put ourselves for a day in the company of one of the wisest and wittiest of them all, the poet Horatius, or "Horace." We will carefully avoid, too, the days of the great circus shows and games, for we wish to see the ordinary every-day life of the Romans, and not that of their festivals.

The Romans are early risers, so we must be up before sunrise, and make our way to the modest little house of the poet, on the hill that lies east of the Forum. There we find Horace already risen, though usually he is apt to rise later than most of the Romans. To-day, however, he is going to pay a morning visit to his friend and neighbor, Mæcenas, so we find him up and dressed by the time that we arrive.

After a light breakfast of bread dipped in wine, and ripe olives, we set out together. As we pass along the narrow streets, we are surprised at the number of people that we meet, though the sun is barely up above the horizon. Some are slaves and servants, hurrying here and there on business of their masters. Others are children on their way to school, with slaves accompanying them, who carry their tablets and satchels. Many, however, are freemen, and are clad in the full-dress toga, which none but a free Roman citizen may wear. These latter persons bustle along with little baskets in their hands and anxious looks upon their faces. They are "clients," we are told, or dependants of great men, who are hurrying to pay their visit of state to their patron at his morning reception; and the little baskets are to fetch away the gifts of food which each day are set out for them in their patron's house.

As we approach the splendid mansion of Mæcenas, with its beautiful gardens, we see many of these clients going into the house before us; and as we enter we find the outer hall and vestibule full of them. Mæcenas is the friend and adviser of Augustus, and his influence in the state is very great; as he is also a liberal and generous man, the number of clients who are dependent on him is quite large. However, we are not worried by the number of these visitors, though they are pushing and shoving to get ahead of one another; for Horace stands on quite a different footing with Mæcenas from them, and is admitted at once to the presence of the master of the house.

We enter with him, and find ourselves in a large and

stately hall, richly ornamented with pictures and statues. There we find Mæcenas receiving the greetings of the more important of his clients, while he advises this one, perhaps, on some point connected with a suit at law, and that one how best to invest his money. As soon as he sees Horace, however, he comes forward with a smile on his face, for he loves Horace and honors him as Rome's greatest poet.

While the two friends talk, we glance about the hall, and admire the graceful marble columns which support the roof. From time to time we catch bits of the conversation between Mæcenas and our guide.

"Nay, Mæcenas," Horace is saying, "though no one is of a nobler family than yourself, you are not one of those who toss up their heads at men of humble birth. If you had been such a person, I should have had no chance of ever gaining your friendship and aid; for my father, as you know, was born a slave, though he gained his freedom. I shall never be ashamed of my father, however, for though he was a poor man on a lean little farm, he guarded me from bad habits and gave me an education fit for a Senator's son."

After some further talk, Horace takes his leave, and we return with him to his little home. As we enter the house we glance at a sun-dial which stands nearby, and see that it is now near the close of the second hour, or about eight o'clock.

In the Forum, the next three hours are the busiest of the day. Now the judges are seated on the judgment benches and listening to the pleas of the orators in this and that suit at law; and now the crowd of idlers is greatest there. But Horace is not interested in such matters; he quietly enters his library, and there he remains, reading and writing, until near midday. Then, a light luncheon of bread, cold meat, fruit and wine is served by the slaves; and after that comes the mid-day rest and nap, which is still common in all warm climates.

HORACE.

In the afternoon, we accompany Horace, once more, as he leaves the house and sets out for the heart of the city. As we stroll along, we see groups of children playing in the shadow of the houses. Here girls are playing what looks very much like our game of "jackstones," except that they use small bones to play it with. Near by, other girls sit with their dolls, singing lullabies to them; and elsewhere we find groups of active boys, playing with nuts in much the same ways that our boys play with marbles.

As we pass the shops where provisions are sold, Horace stops to ask of the slaves, who have the shops in charge, the prices of herbs and bread; and when he comes to the booth of a fortune teller, he stands listening in the crowd for a while, and smiles at the silly folk who believe all the nonsense that is told them. When we reach the Forum, we find it almost deserted; only a few laggards, like ourselves, are to be seen, and they seem to be on their way toward the open ground by the river.

We follow after them, and soon reach the Field of Mars. Here the armies assemble in time of war, and here, too, we see the voting places where the elections are held each year. But it is nothing of this sort that draws the people now. As we look about us, we see everywhere men of all ages—young, old and middle-aged—engaged in games and exercises of some sort; and almost every afternoon, at this time, we could find the same sight. Here men are running, leaping, wrestling, hurling the spear and quoit. Some are practicing feats on horseback; others, armed with heavy shields and stout clubs, are aiming heavy blows at tall posts; and others still are playing games with balls of various kinds and sizes.

For a while Horace takes part in this latter exercise. We join him and throw the ball about until our muscles are tired and our bodies heated with the exercise and the sun. Then, leaving the Field of Mars, we go to refresh ourselves at the baths.

To the Roman, the daily bath was just as important as daily exercise; and many fine and costly buildings, for this purpose, were erected by wealthy men and opened to the people. Some of these came to include within them gardens, columned porches, libraries, and everything that could give one comfort and amusement; and these baths came to be great places of resort for the Roman idlers.

We will go with Horace, however, to one of the smaller and more modest buildings, where baths alone are to be found. There, for a very small sum, we may have a cold swimming bath, a hot-water bath, or a hot-air bath. We make our choice, and after bathing, and rubbing our bodies with olive oil, we find ourselves much refreshed and the weariness gone from our limbs.

VERGIL.

Horace has been invited to dinner, for this evening, to the house of an acquaintance, and we have permission to accompany him there. The water-clocks and sun-dials tell us that it is now nearing the ninth hour, — that is, it is about three o'clock—so we must hasten, as Roman dinners begin in the middle of the afternoon.

When we reach the house, we are at once shown into the dining-room. There we find the little company gathered, and among them we recognize Mæcenas, whose reception we attended in the early morning. Standing with him, we see a man of fine features and bright eyes, whose face lights up as, now and then, in the course of the conversation, he quotes a verse of poetry. This is the poet Vergil, the friend of Horace, whose great poem, on the fall of Troy, called the

Æneid, is still read and enjoyed by scholars the world over.

In the center of the room we see a small table of maple wood, and about three sides of this are arranged couches or sofas on which the guests are to recline during the dinner. When we have taken our places, three on a couch, slaves advance and take the sandals from off our feet, while others hand around silver basins filled with water, for us to wash our hands. For a moment we wonder at this, then we notice that there are no knives and forks on the table, and learn that we are expected to take our food with our fingers; so we see at once the reason for it.

When our hands have been bathed and dried, slaves enter with a tray containing the first course of the dinner. This is placed on the table in front of us, and then we see it consists of a wild boar roasted whole, with eggs, and lettuce, radishes, olives, and other relishes heaped about it. While we are being helped to these dishes, wine mixed with honey is handed about in golden goblets. After this course many others follow,—roast fowls, fresh oysters, fish with strange sauces, blackbirds roasted with their feathers on, pastry made in wonderful shapes, fruits and nuts. And yet this is not a fine banquet, as Roman banquets go; for whole fortunes, at times, are spent by Romans on one entertainment.

Though we took our places at the table at three o'clock, we do not rise from it until near sunset. After the hunger of all is satisfied, basins of water are again passed, and the hands are cleaned after the repast. But the guests still linger about the table, drinking wine weakened with water, playing at games, and engaging in conversation.

As we listen to the talk of the different members of the party, our attention is caught by something that Horace is saying. He is expressing his preference for a life in the country, and saying how much he would rather be at his little farm near Rome, which the generous Mæcenas has given him, than in the bustling city.

"Happy is the man," he says, "who tills his little farm with his own oxen, far away from the noise and hurry of the city. He is neither alarmed by the trumpet which calls the soldier to arms, nor frightened by the storms which cause the merchant to fear for his ships at sea. In the spring he trims his vines, stores his honey, and shears his sheep; and when autumn comes, he gathers his pears and the purple grape. He may lie full length on the matted grass under some old tree, and listen to the warbling of the birds in the woods, and the waters gliding by in their deep channels. And when winter comes, with its rains and snows, he may hunt the wild boar with his hounds, or spread nets to take thrushes, and snares to catch hares and cranes."

At last the company breaks up, just as the sun is setting beyond the Tiber. Then all betake themselves to their homes. As the Romans are early risers, they retire early also. Soon after darkness has fallen upon the earth, the greater part of the people in this vast city are buried in slumber, while the darkness of night is broken only here and there by a glimmer of light which shows that in some belated household a lamp still burns; and so our day in Rome comes to an end.

XXVII

The Empire After Augustus.

WHEN Augustus died, the whole empire mourned for him. As time went on, men mourned for him more bitterly than ever; for it was long before they had another ruler as wise and good as he.

The step-son of Augustus became emperor after him, and he was a cruel tyrant who put men to death upon mere suspicion. And the next emperor was half-mad, and once threatened to have his horse made consul, and at another time raised a great army, and marched it hundreds of miles, and then commanded the soldiers to gather the shells upon the sea-beach and carry them back to Rome. After him came a weak and foolish emperor who allowed the cruelest acts to be committed in his name, and then forgot them, and invited the persons to dinner whom he had just had put to death. And then came an emperor named Nero, who was a monster of vanity and cruelty; he was suspected of setting fire to the city and allowing more than two-thirds of it to burn up, in order that he might rebuild it finer than it had been before.

But even under such rulers, the misgovernment scarcely extended beyond the city of Rome itself, and the distant provinces were more prosperous and happy than they had been during the time when the Senate and the people of Rome ruled over them. For

a hundred years there was no civil war. Then when one did begin, after the death of Nero, it lasted only a short time, and ended by bringing in a set of emperors, almost every one of whom was as strong and as good as Augustus.

Before this civil war, all the emperors who had ruled had been related in some way to the family of Julius Cæsar; but after it, this was no longer the case. The emperors now were usually the leaders of the armies which guarded the different borders of the empire. Like the soldiers whom they commanded, they were often not Romans at all, but had been born and raised in some of the provinces. They did not care so much for the city of Rome and the Romans, therefore; and in course of time the people of Sicily and Spain, and finally of all the provinces, were admitted to have equal rights in the empire with the citizens of Rome itself.

A new plan was found in this period for arranging who should be emperor. The emperor who was ruling would choose the best man he could find, and adopt him as his son; and this son would then share the rule with him while he lived, and would succeed him when he died. In this way the empire had a hundred years of the best rule that it was ever to know. Indeed, the people who dwell about the Mediterranean have never seen, before or since, a time of such unbroken happiness.

One of the emperors who made this time famous, was named Trajan, and he became so great a favorite, that when the Romans wished to pay a compliment to their rulers after this, they could only say that they were "more fortunate than Augustus and better than Trajan." He was a great soldier, and made war upon the people who lived beyond the Danube and conquered some of their territory; but this was soon given up again. To celebrate his victories, Trajan set up in the Forum at Rome, a carved marble column, a hundred and thirty feet high, with his statue on the top. This column still stands at Rome, after eighteen hundred years; and winding around the outside of it may still be traced the carvings which picture scenes from his wars with the tribes along the Danube.

The ruler who followed Trajan was named Hadrian. He was a man of peace, and a great traveler and builder. He visited all the provinces of the empire, from far-off Britain to Egypt and the East; and wherever he went he caused new temples and theatres and other public buildings to be raised, and the old ones to be repaired. And in Britain, he built a great wall across the island from sea to sea, to protect the Roman citizens there against the tribes that lived in what is now Scotland.

The two emperors who came just after Hadrian were different from any that had gone before. They were scholars and wise men, and liked the quiet of their libraries much better than the noise of armies and battles, or the traveling of which Hadrian had been so fond. But they both governed with the single purpose of making the people under their rule as happy as possible; so when it became necessary to make war to defend the empire, they did not hesitate to give up their own desires and march at the head of their armies. This became more and more necessary during the reign of Marcus Aurelius, the second of these two emperors; and finally he met his death on the bank of the river Danube, fighting against the Germans who dwelt along that stream.

MARCUS AURELIUS.

With the death of this great and good emperor, the "golden age" of the empire came to an end. From now on the barbarians pressed more closely on the empire, and it became more difficult to defend it against their attacks. The Romans and the Italians had lost the old bravery and skill in fighting, which had enabled them to conquer the whole world; while the barbarians had learned much about war from their long struggles with Rome. Besides this, the government now fell once more into unworthy hands. Ignorant soldiers gave the rule to men who were not fit for it; and once the position of emperor was even put up at auction and sold to the highest bidder.

So a hundred years of war and bloodshed followed. This did not cease, until at last a strong ruler named Diocletian got the power, and divided the empire into an eastern and western half, each with its own ruler, so that the people might be better defended from the barbarians, and better governed in their own countries. Many other changes were made by Diocletian; then when his work was finished, he resigned his power and spent the rest of his days in quiet, far from the struggles of war and politics.

Soon after Diocletian had resigned his power, a new emperor arose who once more united the rule over both the eastern and western halves of the empire. His name was Constantine, and he is called "the Great." He did two things which were very important. In the first place, he was the first emperor to become a Christian himself, and to allow the Christians to practise their religion openly. In the second place, he moved the capital of the Roman empire to the shores of the Black Sea, and there built a new city which was called from his name, "Constantinople," or "the city of Constantine." Some time after the death of Constantine the empire was again divided into an eastern and a western part; and this time the division was a lasting one. After that there was an empire of the East, with its capital at Constantinople; and an empire of the West, with its capital at Rome.

Meanwhile, the barbarians, especially the Germans, had been growing more and more troublesome. Great hordes of them at last broke through the line of forts along the Rhine and the Danube, and wandered up and down the lands of the empire, plundering and destroying for many years. Battle after battle was fought with them, and sometimes the Germans were the victors, and sometimes the Romans were; but the armies of the emperors were never again strong enough to drive the Germans out of the Roman lands.

Then the Romans tried to buy off the Germans by giving them lands to settle on, and by taking their young men into the Roman armies. But the news of the success of these bands soon brought others after them, all demanding lands within the bounds of the empire. And often they would not wait to ask for a place to settle, but would seize upon it without asking, and the armies of the empire could not prevent it. In this way, Spain, and Gaul, and Britain, and even northern Italy, passed into the hands of the Germans; and in all these lands the Roman rule came to an end forever.

The new city of Constantinople was so well situated and so strongly built that the Germans were never able to capture it; and the empire there went on for a thousand years longer. But the empire of the West was not so strong. The city of Rome had been greatly weakened when Constantine moved the capital of the empire to the Black Sea, and it was not so able to stand the attacks of the barbarians. Just eight hundred years after it had been taken by the Gauls, Rome fell into the hands of the barbarians a second time, and was plundered by a wandering tribe of Germans. Then sixty-six years later, in the year 476 after Christ, one of these German chiefs seized the last

Roman emperor in Italy, and took his crown and scepter from him; and the Roman empire of the West quietly came to an end.

You have seen how the Romans spread their rule from the little district around Rome, until they had gained a vast empire, and now you have seen how that empire was lost. The Romans gained their power because they were worthy to rule, and they lost it because they ceased to be worthy. The rule of Rome, which had at first been a blessing to the world, at last became an injury to it. When that time came, it was easy for the Germanic barbarians to overthrow the old government.

But it is easier to destroy a government than it is to build one up. The Germans were at this time a rude and unlettered people, and they had never lived in cities and were ignorant of many things connected with ruling over them. So it was to take them a long time to set up strong governments which should rule as well as the old Romans had done. In the end, however, they succeeded in doing this; and then the modern nations of Europe arose out of the ruins of the Roman Empire, and united in themselves all that was best of the old Roman civilization, with the newer, freer and better ideas of the Germans.

XXVIII

The Christians and the Empire.

DURING the centuries that the Roman power was slowly weakening and dying, there was another power that was constantly growing stronger. This was the power of the Christian religion. It was to grow until it had conquered the Romans; then it was to conquer the Germans, who overthrew the Roman rule. In this way it was to go on, until it had conquered the world in a far wider sense than Rome had ever done; and at last it was to become the mightiest power that the world has ever seen.

Palestine, the land of the Jews, was first conquered by Pompey, before his war with Cæsar, while he was setting the affairs of the East in order. There Christ was born during the time that Augustus was emperor, and he was put to death in the reign of the emperor who succeeded Augustus. Up to that time the teachings of Christ had not spread beyond that portion of the Jews who accepted them. After his death, however, the Apostles—especially the Apostle Paul—began to spread his teachings among other nations; and soon there were little bands of Christians to be found in many of the cities about the Mediterranean Sea.

Then it began to be a question as to how the Roman government would treat this new religion. Usually the Romans were very tolerant, and allowed the nations that they conquered to worship whatever gods they chose, and even to bring their worship with them to Rome. In this way, the Egyptians and Jews and other eastern nations had been allowed to build temples at Rome and worship their gods there with almost no disturbance.

It was different, however, with the Christians. There were many reasons why the Romans would not let them worship freely. The Jews were very bitter against the Christians, and they informed the Romans that the Christians were guilty of many horrible crimes in their meetings. These charges were not true, of course; but the Romans, and perhaps even the Jews themselves, believed them. Then, too, the Christians were charged with introducing a new and strange god, and with denying that the gods of the empire were gods at all. When the Christians would not offer sacrifice to the Roman gods—especially when they would not worship the statues of the emperors, who were now looked upon as gods—they were charged with rebellion, and with plotting to overthrow the government. And whenever war, or famine, or disease, came upon the people, they were ready to blame it upon the Christians.

"The gods are angry with us for sheltering those who deny them!" they would cry at such times. "The Christians must be put to death! To the lions with the Christians!"

Then all persons who were suspected of being Christians would be seized and hurried off to the judges. If they admitted that they were Christians, they were promptly sentenced to death. If they denied it, they were asked to offer sacrifice to the statue of the emperor; and if they would not do this, that was taken as a sign that the charge was true, and they, too, were declared guilty.

In this way the prisons would be filled with Christians. It made no difference whether they were slaves or free, old or young, strong men or delicate women. Their fate was the same. When next the people were gathered to see the games in the great Circus, the Christians would be driven into the arena. Then lions, and leopards, and other wild beasts would be turned loose upon them, while the cruel Romans shouted and cheered from their seats around about.

The first persecution of the Christians at Rome took place while Nero was emperor. A great fire had broken out and burned more than two-thirds of the city. The Romans believed,—whether rightly or wrongly,—that Nero himself had given order to set the city on fire, so that he might rebuild it in a more splendid style than ever. There were ugly rumors, too, that while the waves of flame were sweeping over the city, Nero had been seen on a tower watching the sight, and unfeelingly singing and playing upon a harp.

The Roman people were, therefore, very angry with Nero, and for a while it looked as though there would be a rebellion. To quiet them, Nero had it reported that it was the Christians who had started the fire, and that while it was burning many of them had been seen going about with torches in their hands and setting fire to buildings which had not yet caught.

This changed the people's wrath from their emperor to the Christians. The cry arose, "To the lions with the Christians"; and many hundreds of them were hurried off to prison without any kind of trial. Nero also invented many new and cruel punishments for them. Some were covered with the skins of wild beasts, and then dogs were set on them. Others were wrapped in sheets of pitch and burned at night in Nero's gardens; and the name of "Nero's candles" was given to these. Others, more mercifully, were put to death in their prisons; and in later days it was said that among this number were the Apostles Peter and Paul.

It was not always, however, the evil emperors like Nero who persecuted the Christians. Sometimes the most severe persecutions were begun by orders of good emperors. They were ignorant of the real teachings of Christ, and believed that the charges made against the Christians were true. In this way it happened that Trajan, and Marcus Aurelius, and Diocletian all persecuted the Christians and had large numbers of them put to death.

The Christians did not burn the bodies of their dead, as the Romans did; they buried them instead. But in place of burying them in cemeteries, such as we all know, they dug out great tunnels and caves in the soft rock, and formed tombs along their sides in which they laid the bodies of their dead. In this way the hills of Rome came to be mined through and through with such tunnels, or "catacombs" as they were called.

At last these catacombs made a great network of passages, miles and miles in length, which crossed and re-crossed one another, under the city, just as the Roman streets did on the surface of the ground above.

When the persecutions would begin, and danger would come, the Christians would hide themselves in these streets of the dead below the surface of the ground; and there, too, they would often hold their church services to comfort one another in their times of trial and distress. These catacombs still exist at Rome, and they are one of the sights that every visitor to that city is sure to want to see.

In these persecutions, many hundreds of Christians were put to death because of their religion; and many more were imprisoned, or suffered in other ways for their faith. But through it all they were brave and glad, for they suffered for Christ as Christ had suffered for them.

The persons who suffered in this way were called "martyrs," which means "witnesses" for the Truth. Many Christians eagerly sought to receive a martyr's death, and mourned when they did not succeed. Even boys and girls became heroes in these persecutions, and endured death without flinching. At Rome a thirteen-year-old girl named Agnes was brought before the judges on the charge of being a Christian. She refused to deny the charge, and was put to death by the sword; and after that her name was honored as that of a saint. And in Gaul, a young slave girl endured the most cruel tortures and at last was thrown to the wild beasts in a net, because she would not give up Christianity; and a boy fifteen years old was also put to death there, at the same time and for the same reason.

One of the noblest of the martyrs was a man named Polycarp, who was put to death in Asia Minor while

Marcus Aurelius was emperor. He was then an old, old man, of ninety years, and all the Christians of the East looked up to him with love and admiration, for he was a disciple of the Apostle John. When the soldiers came to arrest him, their commander took pity on him, and tried to persuade him to sacrifice to the Roman gods, and so save his life.

"What harm can there be in saying 'the emperor, our Lord,' and in offering sacrifices to him?" he asked.

At first Polycarp was silent; but when they went on to urge him, he said mildly:

"I will not do as you advise me."

When he was brought before the Roman governor of that province, he, too, urged him to swear by the emperor as by a god, and give proof of his repentance by saying, with the people, "Away with the godless." But Polycarp looked with a firm eye at the crowd that stood by; then with his eyes lifted up to heaven, and pointing at them with his finger, he cried:

"Away with the godless."

And when the governor urged him further, and said, "Curse Christ, and I will release you;" Polycarp answered:

"Eighty-six years have I served him, and he has done me nothing but good,—and how could I curse him, my Lord and Saviour? If you wish to know what I am, I tell you frankly I am a Christian."

Even then the Roman governor wished to save the brave old man, if he could; but Polycarp would not yield. At last the governor turned to the people, and a herald proclaimed:

"Polycarp has confessed that he is a Christian."

When the people heard these words, they cried out that he was the father of the Christians, that he was the enemy of their gods, and that he had taught many to turn from their worship and cease to sacrifice in their temples. They demanded that Polycarp should be burned at the stake, and they themselves brought wood for this purpose from the workshops and baths. Then the Roman governor gave his consent, and it was done as they had desired; and Polycarp met his death with the same steadfastness and courage which he had shown at his trial.

In this way men and women of all classes, young and old, noble and slave, suffered and were put to death. But still the number of the Christians increased with each persecution.

"Go on," said one of the Christian writers to the Roman rulers; "go on,—torture us and grind us to dust. Our numbers increase more rapidly than you mow us down. The blood of the martyrs is the seed of the Church."

At last the time came when the persecutions were to cease altogether, and the emperors themselves, and all of their officers were to become Christians.

This happened, as you have already seen, while Constantine was on the throne. During the first part of his reign, he had to struggle against several rivals in the empire. At one time, the story goes, while he was marching rapidly from Gaul into Italy to attack one of his enemies, he saw a flaming cross in the sky in broad day, and on the cross were these words:

"In this sign, conquer."

In the battle which followed, Constantine did conquer; and he believed that he owed his victory to the god of the Christians. So one of the first things that he did after that was to issue an order to stop the persecutions, and permit the Christians to practise their religion openly and in peace.

After this, Constantine became a Christian himself, and did all that he could to favor their cause. Temples were taken away from the priests of the old gods and given to the Christians to use as churches; and only Christians were appointed to offices under the empire. And when Constantine died, his sons followed the same religion; and the number of the Christians grew rapidly under them. And though Julian, the nephew of Constantine, ceased to be a Christian when he became emperor, and tried to bring the people back to the worship of Mars and Jupiter once more, he did not succeed. The task was too great for him. After him, all of the emperors were Christians; and at last a time came when the old worship was put down altogether.

Then the altars of the old gods were thrown down and their images were broken; and the sacred fire in the temple of Vesta, which had burned without interruption for eleven centuries, was extinguished forever. And after that all persons were punished who dared to sacrifice to the old gods who had so long been worshiped by the Roman people.

XXIX

The Remains of Rome.

THE Roman Empire came to an end many centuries ago, but there is still much of Rome left in the world to-day. The Romans live for us yet in their history, and also in the languages and laws of Europe, which are founded in large part upon the language and law of Rome. In another way also Rome and the life of her citizens are with us still. The Roman roads and bridges and walls can still be traced all over Europe, and at Rome a few great buildings remain which give us a faint idea of the grandeur of the ancient city. Moreover, by a strange chance, a Roman city— the city of Pompeii—has been preserved for us entire, very much as it was toward the close of the first century after Christ; and in this we can draw near to the life of the people of Rome as it must have been eighteen hundred years ago.

You will remember, perhaps, that the Romans of the time of Cincinnatus lived partly in the country upon their farms, and partly in the city. Although the Romans of the empire were very different in their thoughts and tastes from those of the earlier days, they were like them in this, that they did not confine themselves to a life in Rome. Every citizen who was able to afford it, had a house outside of Rome,—on some beautiful Italian lake, at the foot of the mountains, or on the seashore. The western coast of Italy was lined, in places, with the country houses, or villas, of the Romans; and one beautiful bay—that on which the city of Naples stands—was noted for the number of the towns and villas which covered its shores.

Overlooking this bay, at the present time, is the lofty peak of Mt. Vesuvius. Travelers who visit the city of Naples to-day think themselves fortunate if they are there during an eruption of Vesuvius; for it is now one of the most active volcanoes of the world. Up to the first century after Christ, however, the Romans knew nothing of Vesuvius as an active volcano. Cities were built at its very foot; and one of the Roman writers describes Vesuvius as rising behind these towns, "well cultivated and inhabited all around, except the top, which is for the most part level and entirely barren, ashy to the view, and displaying great hollows in rocks which look as if they had been eaten by fire. So we may suppose this spot," he continues, "to have been a volcano formerly, with burning craters, which are now extinguished for want of fuel."

In the year 79 A.D., the fires of Vesuvius burst forth again, after their long, long rest, and brought destruction to the country around it.

It was the afternoon of a November day, and the burning heats of summer were now past. Many of the Roman visitors had left their country homes, and returned to the capital. Some, however, still lingered in their beautiful villas; and such of them as were not taking their afternoon nap, were reading, or busying themselves with other matters. In the cities near by, life was going on as usual. In one place masons were at work repairing a damaged building; in the Forum, the shop-keepers were showing their wares to customers; in the crowded theatre men and women watched with wolfish eyes the struggles of the gladiators.

Suddenly a strange cloud, shaped like a pine-tree, with a lofty trunk and a cluster of branches at the top, was seen to rise above Vesuvius. As the people watched it, it continually changed in height; and sometimes it was fiery-bright in appearance, and sometimes it seemed streaked with black.

This was the beginning of a great eruption of dust and ashes, which lasted for days, and is said to have scattered its showers of volcanic dust as far as Africa and Egypt. At the same time, the land was shaken by earthquakes, and the sea drew back from the shore.

The people, in terror, fled in all directions, by sea and land, thinking the end of the world had come. Most of them escaped in safety, but some, who tried to brave the storm and remain in the cities, were lost.

When the eruption had ceased, it was found that a thick layer of ashes and mud was spread over the country around, and the towns which were nearest to the mountain were covered so deeply that only the tops of the tallest buildings were visible above the surface of the ground. As the years went by, other eruptions came, and added to the thickness of this covering. Then the top layer was gradually changed to a fine loam; and grass, and bushes, and even trees, sprang up and covered the spot where the cities lay buried. At last they seemed wholly lost to the memory of man.

For sixteen hundred years the cities about Mount Vesuvius then lay buried and lost to view. Then a well, deeper than usual, happened to be dug in the ground above one of them. There, many feet under ground, ancient statues were found, and bits of sculptured marble. Search was made, and it was found that the well had struck the stage of a buried theatre. Then scholars began to remember the story of the destruction of the cities so long ago; and they began to dig elsewhere also.

From that time to this, the work of uncovering the buried cities has slowly been going on. Several museums are now filled with the pictures, statues and household furniture which have been taken from beneath the ashes of Vesuvius. The town which has been most thoroughly examined is Pompeii, of which over one-half has been uncovered. There we of the nineteenth century can see the houses and streets of the first century after Christ, very much as they were left when the citizens fled in fear for their lives through the showers of falling stones and ashes.

The removal of the covering over Pompeii has shown that the city had a forum, surrounded by temples and law courts, and other public buildings; and this, as at Rome, was the most splendid part of the city. But it is not for the public buildings of Pompeii that we care most: ancient temples, and other public buildings, as well preserved as these, may be found in other places. But the glimpse which we get into the private houses of the town, and into the life of the people in the streets and shops,—this we can get nowhere else and it is this which makes our interest in Pompeii so great.

Let us leave the Forum, then, and go down one of the many streets that lead from it through the town. The first thing that strikes us is the narrowness of the streets. In some of the broadest of them, two chariots could scarcely have passed each other; and some of the ways are so narrow as not even to allow of the passage of one. The pavements are formed of large pieces of

A STREET IN POMPEII.

stone, joined together with great care; and the ruts worn by the passing wheels can still be seen in some of them. On each side of the street is a narrow walk for the foot passengers; this is raised above the level of the roadway, and large stepping-stones are placed in the middle of the street to enable the people to cross from one side to the other in rainy weather.

Passing along one of these streets, we notice that the

houses are built out to the edge of the pavement, and have their plain and unadorned side toward the passers-by. They are built,—as are the houses in many countries to-day,—about one or more inner courts into which most of the rooms open. Often the street side was occupied by shops which were rented out by the owner of the house, and which had no connection with the life of the house itself.

Let us enter one of these houses, and see how a Roman dwelling was arranged. We will choose one of the larger and finer buildings. The entrance is through a passage-way which lies between two of the shops which make up the front of the house. There we find the Latin word for "Welcome" formed of bits of stone, in the mosaic work of the floor. Stepping over this, we enter first the large public hall, which you see plainly in the picture on page 250. Here the master of the house received the visitors who came to see him on business, or to pay their respects to him. If they came from a distance, they might be lodged over night in the small rooms which you see opening off from the hall on each side. The walls of this large room were decorated with paintings and drawings, and here and there we see places where the statues shown in the picture once stood. The floor here, and, indeed, all through the lower story of the house, was formed of blocks of marble or other stone, and usually the blocks were of different colors and were arranged to form a pattern of some sort.

In the centre of the floor of the room which we are examining, we see a square basin, several feet deep. When we ask what this was for, we are told that there was an opening in the roof above this, and that the basin was to catch the water which fell when it rained. Unfortunately, the roofs of the houses have all been broken down or burned, and the rooms are now open to the sky; so we have to imagine this opening in the roof. In the beginning, we are told, it was left to let out the smoke and vapors from the fires; for none of the houses had chimneys, and the fireplaces were only metal pots or pans in which charcoal might be burned. We could not imagine ourselves, in our cold climate,

A ROMAN HOUSE.

living with such an opening over our heads; but in the warmer climate of Italy, this plan had many advantages. For one thing, the rooms were thus freely ventilated; and an awning, drawn across the opening, served to keep out the sun in summer.

Leaving the public hall, we come through another passage to the private part of the house, where the women and children dwelt, and where no visitor might come without a special invitation from the master.

Here we find another court, with rows of slender, graceful columns about it. Opening off this court, are small low bedrooms, which we should think very uncomfortable; and here, too, is the dining-room, where the master of the house entertained his friends at dinner. Above this court, also, there was an opening in the roof, with a basin below to catch the water; and about the basin, between and behind the columns, there grew, perhaps, beds of blooming flowers and clumps of evergreens.

Only the ground floor remains of most of the houses of Pompeii; but there must have been a second story to all of the better houses, and sometimes even a third story. But the upper part of the house was for the use of the slaves and the dependants of the family, and could not have been so well arranged, nor so beautiful, as the lower portion.

Even if we had been the first, after its discovery, to examine this house, we should not have found the walls hung with framed pictures, as with us. Instead of that, we might, perhaps, have found its walls beautifully decorated with scenes and designs painted on the wall itself, which had kept their colors almost fresh in the darkness of the buried city. Some of these pictures have now been allowed to fade by exposure to the light and air; but many have been carefully taken down and preserved in the museums.

When these houses were first uncovered, many pieces of furniture were found in them; but according to our ideas, the Roman rooms must have seemed rather bare for living rooms. We should have found in them only a few chairs, some small tables, three couches in the dining-room—you will remember that the Romans reclined at their meals—some beds or couches in the bedrooms, and here and there high stands for their queer oil lamps. The form of these articles, however, was often most elegant; and at times they were made of very rich material and with great skill of workmanship. Besides such larger pieces of furniture, many smaller articles have been found, as the work of unearthing the city has gone on. Among these, we may name cooking vessels, vases, cups and fine glasses, combs, hairpins, polished metal mirrors, and many pieces of jewelry.

SPOONS FROM POMPEII.

Besides the private houses, and the public buildings, many shops have been found in Pompeii. Most of these are just tiny little rooms in the front of the houses, and are entirely open toward the street. Usually we can tell what sort of a shop each is by the sign in front of it. Here is one with a wooden goat before it, and we know that it was a milk shop. Another has a large jar as a sign, and we know at once that it was a wine shop. The one with a snake before it was a drug store; and this one with a row of hams for a sign, we are told, was an eating house. Three bakeries have been discovered, and these give us a very good idea of how the bread of the

DRINKING BOWL FROM POMPEII.

Romans looked; for in the oven of one of them, eighty-three loaves were discovered, black and charred, but still keeping their original shape. A washing and dyeing shop, for the care of the woolen garments which were almost the only kind worn, has also been discovered; and here the stone tubs may still be seen waiting for their contents, while on the walls are pictures of men standing in tubs and stamping with their feet, to show us how they were used in washing garments.

In one way the people of Pompeii were very much like some bad boys of our own day. They loved to scratch and write on the walls of the houses of the town,—which, indeed, must have offered tempting chances to all by being so near to the sidewalk. So here, we find verses from the poets; and there, letters of the Greek alphabet, scratched by boys too small to reach high up on the walls. In many places advertisements are scratched in the plaster of the walls, and announcements of fights of gladiators, and performances in the theatre. Occasionally, too, we find pictures like the one shown on page 254, where a gladiator is seen coming down the steps of the amphitheatre, with a palm leaf of victory in his right hand. Such drawings and inscriptions are often found on the ancient buildings of Rome also. There, as at Pompeii, they must have been the work of the

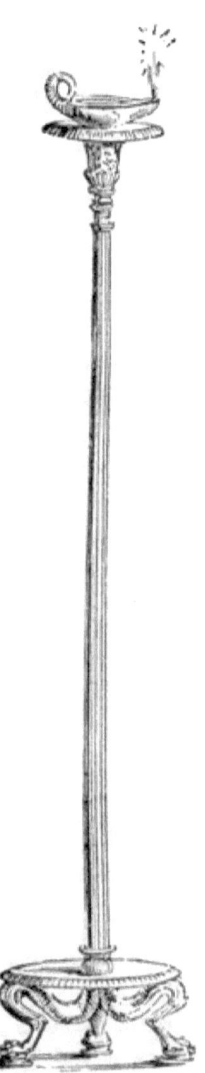

LAMP AND STAND.

common people and the young boys, for the writers are usually very uncertain of their grammar and spelling.

The old Roman life has been kept for us better in the city of Pompeii than anywhere else; for at Rome itself, the buildings and furniture and tools and ornaments of the people, did not remain unused and unchanged during the centuries. People continued to live in the greater city, through all the changes that the years brought with them; and they live there to this day. Only a few of the great monuments of the past, however, remain among them.

DRAWING ON THE OUTER WALL OF A HOUSE IN POMPEII

Do you wonder how the magnificent buildings of the older Rome, which were so solidly built of stone and marble, could have been so nearly destroyed, even in so long a stretch of time?

For many hundreds of years after the Roman empire of the West had come to an end, the people of the city knew little of the past, and cared still less about it. They used the old temples for churches, changing them to suit their purposes; and they tore down the finest buildings of the older city, in order to get stone for use in building new ones of their own. There is no doubt that, in this way, the Romans themselves have done more harm to the old city than all the armies that have ever captured Rome. If we could only learn the history and the former use of each of the marbles, stones and bricks, of which the palaces and churches of modern Rome are built, our knowledge of the city of the Cæsars would be almost complete.

In the fifteenth century the Church of St. Peter, the grandest in the world to-day, was begun at Rome, and rose slowly for more than two hundred years before it reached completion. The building of this church alone caused more destruction to the remains of ancient Rome than the ten centuries of ignorance that had gone before. Of the huge masses of marble of every color and size used in it, not an inch was dug from the quarries in modern times. They were all taken from the ancient buildings, many of which were leveled to the ground for the sake of one or two pieces only. At this time, also, the greatest sculptors that Italy has ever seen were flourishing; and they too found marbles ready to their hand in the fallen columns of the ancient temples. In this way, the materials of the most beautiful Christian chapel in the world, were taken from the tomb of the Emperor Hadrian.

If you ever go to Rome, and see the great arching dome of St. Peter's, and the other beautiful sights of the modern city, you must remember this. The new Rome which the eye sees contains the Rome of ancient times beneath its soil and in its greatest buildings, in something of the same way in which our language holds the old Latin words which have been worked over into a different form, and put to different uses in our speech. At first glance we see only that which is new, and we think that the old has completely perished; but, as we look closer and study into things, we find that all of the past is there also, if we only know how to find it.

SUMMARIES OF CHAPTERS.

I.—The Peninsula of Italy.

1. Position, size, and shape; comparison with Greece and Spain.
2. Climate.
3. Surface: the valley of the River Po; the Apennine mountains; the plains.
4. Rivers: general character; the River Tiber.
5. Coast lands: in the northwest; about the mouth of the Tiber; in the south; the eastern coast; the lands about the mouth of the Po.
6. Early governments in Italy; the city of Rome.

II.—Romulus and the Beginning of Rome.

1. Difficulty of learning how and when Rome was founded; the belief of the Romans.
2. Early life of Romulus.
3. Founding of the city.
4. Seizure of the Sabine women; war; the Sabines settle at Rome.
5. The rule of Romulus.
6. His disappearance.

III.—Numa, the Peaceful King.

1. Election of Numa.
2. His character and policy.
3. The Roman religion; the gods Jupiter, Mars, Juno, Minerva, Vesta, and Janus.
4. The worship of the gods arranged by Numa: the Vestal Virgins; the dancing priests of Mars.
5. Death of Numa.

IV.—The Last of the Kings.

1. New wars: their lesson for the Romans; Alba Longa destroyed.

2. New walls; sewers; the temple on the Capitol.
3. The Sybilline books.
4. Tarquin the Proud, the seventh king.
5. Tarquin driven out, and a republic set up.

V.—The War with Lars Porsena.

1. **Plot of** the young nobles to restore Tarquin; the judgment of Brutus.
2. Lars Porsena aids Tarquin.
3. Horatius at the Bridge.

VI.—The Stories of Mucius and Clœlia.

1. The story of Mucius.
2. Lars Porsena makes peace.
3. The story of Clœlia.
4. The last war with Tarquin; Castor and Pollux.

VII.—Secession of the Plebeians.

1. Patricians and plebeians.
2. The grievances of the plebeians.
3. Struggles **between** the classes.
4. The secession to the Sacred Mount.
5. **Tribunes appointed to protect the** plebeians.
6. Continued struggles.

VIII.—The Story of Coriolanus.

1. **Early life of Caius** Marcius.
2. How he gained the name Coriolanus.
3. His struggle with the plebeians; he is sent into exile.
4. He leads the Volscians against Rome.
5. Rome saved by Veturia.

IX.—The Family of the Fabii.

1. Roman families.
2. The Fabii and the plebeians.
3. The Fabii march against the Veientians.
4. Destruction of the Fabii.

X.—THE VICTORY OF CINCINNATUS.

1. The wars with the Æquians.
2. A Roman army entrapped.
3. Cincinnatus made Dictator.
4. His victory over the Æquians.
5. Cincinnatus lays down his power.

XI.—THE LAWS OF THE TWELVE TABLES.

1. The early Roman law; grievances of the people.
2. Struggle to have the laws made public.
3. The "Ten Men" chosen.
4. The Twelve Tables published.
5. Their provisions.
6. Growth of the Roman law; its influence.

XII.—HOW CAMILLUS CAPTURED VEII.

1. Rome's wars with Veii; the long siege.
2. The Alban lake and the oracle of Apollo.
3. Draining the Alban lake.
4. Camillus captures Veii.
5. Removal of the gods to Rome.
6. Camillus and the treacherous schoolmaster.
7. Camillus quarrels with the people; his exile.

XIII.—THE COMING OF THE GAULS.

1. The home of the Gauls.
2. Their appearance and manner of fighting.
3. Settlement of the Gauls in northern Italy.
4. The Gauls before Clusium; action of the Roman ambassadors.
5. The Gauls march upon Rome.
6. The battle; defeat and flight of the Romans.

XIV.—THE GAULS IN ROME.

1. Dismay in the city; the Roman plans.
2. The Gauls enter Rome; the old men in the Forum.
3. Slaughter of the old men; burning of the city.
4. Siege of the Capitol.

5. Camillus's victory over a band of the Gauls; the messenger to the Senate.
6. The attempt of the Gauls to surprise the Capitol; its failure.
7. The Gauls agree to depart from Rome; their terms.

XV.—Rebuilding the City.

1. Despair of the people; proposal to remove to Veii.
2. Speech of Camillus.
3. Decision to remain at Rome.
4. Rebuilding the city.
5. Wars with the neighboring peoples; victories of Camillus.
6. The last war of Camillus; his noble spirit.
7. Death of Camillus; his services to Rome.

XVI.—The New Rome

1. Recovery of Rome from her misfortunes.
2. End of the struggle between the plebeians and patricians.
3. The building of aqueducts.
4. Roman roads; the Appian Way.
5. What Rome learned from other nations.
6. Devotion of the Romans to their city: the story of Marcus Curtius; the sacrifice of Decius Mus.

XVII.—The War with Pyrrhus.

1. The Greeks of Southern Italy.
2. Rome's quarrel with Tarentum.
3. Tarentum calls in King Pyrrhus.
4. The first battle with Pyrrhus; the Roman and the Greek modes of fighting; defeat of the Romans.
5. Embassy of Cinias to Rome; speech of Appius Claudius.
6. Fabricius and Pyrrhus.
7. Second battle with Pyrrhus; the Romans again defeated.
8. Pyrrhus in Sicily.
9. The third battle; victory of the Romans; Pyrrhus leaves Italy.
10. Capture of Tarentum; Rome the ruler of the peninsula.

XVIII.—Rome and the Carthaginians.

1. The Carthaginians: their mother-country; their voyages; their inventions; the city of Carthage.
2. Rivalry with Rome in Sicily; beginning of the first war.
3. Strength of the two peoples.
4. The Romans build a fleet; the "crows"; Roman victories.
5. Regulus in Africa; his capture.
6. Embassy of Regulus to Rome; his death.
7. Length of the war; Roman misfortunes.
8. The Romans build a new fleet; its victory.
9. The treaty of peace.

XIX.—The War with Hannibal.

1. Civil war at Carthage; Hamilcar.
2. Hamilcar goes to Spain; the oath of Hannibal.
3. Carthage conquers Spain; Hannibal becomes commander of the army.
4. Beginning of the second war between Rome and Carthage.
5. Hannibal's plans.
6. His march across the Alps.
7. Arrival in Italy; his successes.
8. Roman fear of Hannibal.
9. Causes of Hannibal's failure; his recall.
10. Scipio Africanus; defeat of Hannibal at Zama.
11. Terms of peace.
12. Last years of Hannibal; his death.

XX.—Rome Conquers the World.

1. Rome's gains from Carthage.
2. Conquest of Northern Italy and Southern Gaul.
3. Conquest of Macedonia.
4. The Romans in Asia Minor and in Egypt.
5. The third war with Carthage; destruction of the city; Roman power in Africa.
6. Good results of Roman rule.
7. Effects of the conquests on the Roman generals; on the common soldiers.

8. Æmilius Paullus; his reforms; his victories over Macedonia; his just dealings.
9. The triumph of Æmilius.

XXI.—The Gracchi and their Mother.

1. Roman marriage customs.
2. Marriage of Tiberius Gracchus and Cornelia, daughter of Scipio Africanus; death of Gracchus; Cornelia and her children.
3. Young Tiberius Gracchus; his service in the army.
4. Troubles of the Roman farmers; slavery; decay of the people.
5. Tiberius Gracchus elected tribune; he attempts to cure these evils.
6. Mistakes of Tiberius; he is put to death; character of the new party struggles at Rome.
7. Caius Gracchus; his election as tribune; his reforms; his death.
8. Conduct of Cornelia.

XXII.—The Wars of Caius Marius.

1. Caius Marius; the eagle's nest; the saying of Scipio Æmilianus.
2. Marius and the war against Jugurtha; his first consulship.
3. The invasion of the Germans.
4. Victories of Marius over the Germans.
5. Marius's sixth consulship; his failure as a statesman.
6. Civil war between the parties of Marius and Sulla.
7. The victories of Sulla; wanderings of Marius; departure of Sulla.
8. Return of Marius to Rome; his cruelties; his seventh consulship and death.
9. Return of Sulla; his terrible vengeance; sufferings of Italy.

XXIII.—Cicero, the Orator.

1. Birth of Cicero; his home life and training.
2. Roman schools; Cicero's life till he was fifteen.
3. Cicero in the law-courts.
4. His first case; his fear of Sulla's anger; travels in Greece.
5. Cicero enters politics; trial of Verres.

6. His election as consul; Catiline's conspiracy.
7. Evils of Roman government; Cicero's plans.
8. New civil wars; Cicero's course.
9. Cicero's death; his character.

XXIV.—Julius Cæsar, the Conqueror of Gaul.

1. Cæsar's youth; Sulla wishes to put him to death.
2. Cæsar in the East; his first training in war.
3. His adventure with the pirates.
4. Cæsar at Rome; his habits.
5. Cæsar made overseer of the public games.
6. Character of the games: the chariot races; the wild beast hunts; the gladiatorial combats.
7. Cæsar and Pompey; Cæsar elected consul, and made governor of Gaul.
8. Condition of Gaul.
9. Cæsar's victory over the Swiss.
10. His march against the Germans; trouble with his soldiers.
11. Extent of his conquests; expeditions into Germany and Britain.
12. Cæsar's character as a general.

XXV.—Cæsar and the Beginning of the Empire.

1. Failure of the government of Rome; the remedy.
2. Pompey joins the party of the Senate; plans against Cæsar.
3. Cæsar crosses the Rubicon; the second civil war begins.
4. Flight of Pompey to Greece; Cæsar goes to Spain.
5. Cæsar follows Pompey to Greece; defeat and death of Pompey.
6. Further conquests of Cæsar; mutiny of his soldiers.
7. Cæsar's four-fold triumph.
8. Cæsar as Emperor; his reforms.
9. Plot against Cæsar; his death.
10. His character.

XXVI.—Rome in the Time of Augustus.

1. Struggles after Cæsar's death; his nephew becomes Emperor.
2. The good rule of Augustus; boundaries of the Empire.
3. Literature under Augustus; the poet Horace.

4. A day in Rome: clients and the morning reception; **the business in the Forum**; the mid-day rest; exercise **in the Field of Mars**; the baths; the banquet.

XXVII.—THE EMPIRE AFTER AUGUSTUS.

1. The successors of Augustus; Nero.
2. The Good Emperors: Trajan; Hadrian; Marcus Aurelius.
3. Decline of the Empire; danger from the Germans; the emperor Diocletian.
4. Constantine the Great; the Christian religion; Constantinople.
5. Division of the Empire; attacks of the Germans; fall of the Empire of the West.
6. The German conquest paves the way for modern Europe.

XXVIII.—THE CHRISTIANS AND THE EMPIRE.

1. Spread of Christianity in the Empire.
2. Attitude of the government; "To the lions with the Christians!"
3. **Persecution** under Nero.
4. The Catacombs.
5. **Bravery of the** Martyrs; Polycarp.
6. **Failure of** the persecutions to check the growth of Christianity.
7. **The** Empire becomes Christian; **Constantine**; end of the old religion.

XXIX.—THE REMAINS OF ROME.

1. Roman remains: language, laws, ruins.
2. Eruption of Vesuvius, 79 A. D.
3. Discovery of the buried cities; Pompeii.
4. Streets and public buildings of Pompeii.
5. The private dwellings.
6. Pictures and furniture.
7. Pompeiian shops.
8. Writings on the walls.
9. Disappearance of the ancient remains at Rome.
10. The old in the new.

www.ingramcontent.com/pod-product-compliance
Lightning Source LLC
Chambersburg PA
CBHW032144230426
43672CB00011B/2447